Truth & Dare

INSIDE OUT MARKETING

Stacey Ruth

Book Layout ©2016 BookDesignTemplates.com

Ordering Information:
Quantity sales. Special discounts are available on quantity purchases by corporations, associations, and others. For details, contact the "Special Sales Department" at info@staceyruthsays.com.

Truth & Dare: Inside Out Marketing/ Stacey Ruth. —1st ed.
ISBN 978-0-6928462-7-8

Contents

To David Ogilvy who said,
"99% of advertising rarely sells anything."

Advertising is based on one thing, happiness. And you know what happiness is? Happiness is the smell of a new car. It's freedom from fear. It's a billboard on the side of the road that screams reassurance that whatever you're doing is okay. You are okay.

—DON DRAPER, AMC's MAD MEN

CHAPTER 1

Mad Men, Liars & Fools

I am a marketer, and I'm not here to sell you anything. Of course, for many people those two ideas thoroughly incompatible. That is because with hundreds of definitions of marketing floating around out there – most of them focused on selling – there is no real agreement about what marketing really is. According to Peter Drucker, *"Marketing is not only much broader than selling, it is not a specialized activity at all. It encompasses the entire business. It is the whole business seen from the point of view of the final result, that is, from the customer's point of view. Concern and responsibility for marketing must therefore permeate all areas of the enterprise."*

While most of us appreciate Peter's wisdom, we resist it too, because it does not get us any closer to what 99% of companies want to do – sell more stuff now! No matter who you are, the size of your business, the previous marketing success you have either enjoyed or longed for – you are hoping to find some fresh marketing insights here, but you also have some degree of skepticism.

Since I just admitted that I'm a marketer, this often puts me in the same league as scam artists and snake oil salesmen for many readers. Scammers are in business at the expense of others' well being, not because of it. They manipulate the fears and play to the ignorance their customers, leaving a trail of confusion, resentment and mistrust wherever they have been, unable to return to the same well ever again, because theirs is a raze and burn business model.

Like several other professions battling a perception problem – for example, realtors, investment brokers, attorneys, agents – where money stakes are high, and results are never guaranteed – marketers are often seen as a shady group. As a result there are those who try to self-market (often identifiable by the phrase: *I can't do any worse than that last agency!)* and those who change agencies every two or three years, always looking for a fresh solution that will generate faster sales and profit.

However, what decades of marketing experience have shown me is that despite the vague sense that most, if not all, marketers are disingenuous; there is still a deep and unshakeable belief that marketing itself really does work. Companies believe they get what they pay for, but rarely do they believe they can afford what it costs. Somewhere there must be an idea so creative and targeted that it will do for them what they cannot do for themselves, and what no one else has been able to do either – break through the noise and the indifference and catapult them to the next level.

Company after company echoes the same anxious refrain: *If only we could find the magic integrated strategy or better understand our customers, or put our spend into creating loyalty instead of desire, or make our brand more appealing to Gen Y, or get this out faster than the competition – then we would be the industry leader, successful and respected by our peers, the stuff of business legends, and retire wealthy at an early age. Can you help us?*

Just like the consumers who eagerly line up to buy every advertised diet fad by the scores, companies keep looking for the magic marketing pill to make them attractive to more customers. They have drunk their own Kool-Aid.

Like the fad diet pill's testimonials there are enough other companies with wild success stories to prove it is possible to stand out in advertising and marketing – and it is (we'll get to this later.) However, you cannot stand out by doing the same thing everyone else is doing. It just doesn't work that way. Yet that is exactly what most companies are trying to do.

The Mad Men

According to Albert Einstein, the definition of insanity is doing the same thing over and over again and expecting different results. Yet that is exactly what happens in ad agencies and corporate marketing departments all over the world. So if you feel like your marketing seems oddly familiar – whether it is direct mail, social, content marketing or experiential – it probably is.

There is a pervasive "me-tooism" in marketing. It is really quite disturbing if you pay attention to the trends. This practice is reactionary and irrational at its best, and dangerously damaging at its worst. In every case the goal is always to stand out and differentiate. What's fascinating is that only rarely does any company become so audacious as to do the thing they claim to want more than anything else; break ranks and actually be unique. Instead they put their logo, their font, their tagline and their corporate copy (that strangely echoes their competitors) into the popular media of the moment. If someone just experienced a dramatic success by engaging through social media then suddenly everyone just simply must be there too – and quickly, before their competitors can. Viral marketing, guerilla marketing, experiential marketing, digital push marketing, meme marketing, and now a resurgence of traditional print marketing – all have been hailed as the missing link to success at some point. Each have scores of books, blogs and pundits to tell you exactly how to execute them successfully – which means becoming highly visible beyond the hundreds and thousands of others doing exactly the same thing. This is why so few companies actually do become highly visible. If we all stand out exactly the same, then none of us stands out at all. What is missing is actual differentiation, and media channels cannot create it for precisely the reasons listed above.

But the me-tooism isn't limited to media channels. It festers deep inside the company messaging. I cannot count the times a client (both entrepreneurial and enterprise) has sat with us in the initial input session for their rebranding strategy and when we ask them, "What makes your company so different from you competitors?" they answer with one or more of the following nine answers:

1. Our exceptional customer service/customer experience
2. Our leading edge technology
3. Our value
4. Our expertise (often in a specific niche)
5. Our people
6. Our size
7. Our effectiveness/results
8. Our speed/efficiency/responsiveness
9. Our patented product/solution/process

Without question, these answers are all excellent characteristics for a company to have. The problem is that an unfortunate number of companies don't have them – especially the customer service. However, I would propose that these are still not unique differentiators. They are just easy, surface answers to a far deeper question. They are parroting back what a customer survey has said, or an article told them was important, and not yet looking fearlessly at where they are, how they got there and whether it is even where they want to be, or, most importantly where they wish to be headed. To address that, later in this book we will explore what a true differentiator looks like, how to dig deep enough to find it, and how it can be leveraged effectively.

These same individuals I mentioned earlier also are extremely proud of their efforts in marketing and branding their company to this point. They are very emotionally invested in the company's marketing, whether they did it themselves, their department did it, or an outside agency did it. They have identified with their marketing as who they are.

I ask them, "So what help would you like from us?" The answer essentially is some variation on, "We need help taking it to the next level." Rarely do they like the response, "Then to reach the next level, you have to completely leave the level you are on." They really aren't as ready as they claim. The list of objections is long; including such things as the impossbility of getting every key stakeholder's buy in on any truly new direction, to lengthy explanations of the complexity of their business model that prohibits any paradigm shifting.

In metaphysics, there is a saying, "Where there is a willingness, there is a way. And where there is willfulness, there is a wall." This wall is the hallmark of companies who keep trying to force the same solution to yield a different result. These companies would do well to examine their strategies in the light of how willing they are to even consider another approach when the wall appears. The result when they just keep ramming the wall is as anyone less emotionally vested in the process would expect – no real shift at all except one gigantic headache.

In actuality, what these companies really want is to *not* take it to another level. A whole new level is absolutely terrifying to them. New levels might have new rules of behavior. It is too daring. Too risky. What they want is a cosmetic, skin-deep solution that validates their current approach and beliefs, or simply the job security of showing activity and forward movement.

Although I am certain my agency is not remotely alone in recognizing the Emporer's frequent lack of clothes, we have all been known to keep our own counsel, bite our tongues when we see the conversation is over, and get to work providing the things these stuck clients ask for, hoping they will ultimately grow bold enough to take the plunge and look inside their business – not just at the marketing veneer – and, happily, occasionally they do.

The Liars

According to recent *Harvard Business Review* and *Brandweek* articles, I'm certainly not the only one wondering why marketers don't market and advertise. If you
believe in your product, why wouldn't you use it? If you want to demonstrate the success of your agency's creative and research prowess, why wouldn't you strut your stuff and watch the clients roll in?

Agencies are fast to remind us that the reason is because theirs is a business-to-business model, not a business-to-consumer one and – well – different rules apply! However, advertisers still sell advertising in droves to those business-to-business companies such as Siemens and FedEx. They sell them on the principle of the importance of brand awareness, and that we are all more likely to buy from someone we have heard of than a complete unknown – which is absolutely true. It is just a bit disconcerting that the advertisers aren't using advertising the way they are touting to their customers. Even more disconcerting is that customers seem oblivious to this little fact, and are all too happy to overlook it.

Other theories about the mysterious lack of advertiser advertising include the saying "the cobbler's children have no shoes," which, as an explanation, is more capable of substantiation, especially when you are talking about smaller firms that are building a base, working hands-on and long hours to execute for their existing clients – which often followed them from their previous agency.

Yet, again, something feels more than a little hypocritical here, since these same agencies, both large and small, are beating the drum of 'invest 4% of your company's earnings back into marketing and advertising' and the importance of advertising to long term growth. That would lead one to deduce that since these same agencies are investing less than 1% (and even in the larger firms, like Deutsch and Ogilvy, closer to .01% of their earnings back into marketing of any kind – *including* PR, public speaking, sponsorship, and awards – never mind advertising specifically – these agencies must have all the work they need and want in perpetuity, or believe they have reached a ceiling for growth through which they can never expand. They are so good, in fact, that there is nowhere left to go. They have arrived.

The truth is that there is a dirty little secret of which most advertisers and CMOs alike are unhappily keenly aware. Now that they can actually measure the ROI (return on investment) results metrics for specific campaigns and tactics, the results are coming back sickeningly poor – universally. According to *Brandweek,* "Copernicus Marketing Consulting has collected performance data on more than 500 marketing programs for consumer and B2B products and services. The firm has found that 84% of these programs are decidedly second-rate, resulting in declining brand equity and market share. Customer satisfaction averages just 74%; most acquisition efforts fail to reach breakeven; no more than 10% of new products succeed; most sales promotions are unprofitable; and advertising ROI is below 4%."

This same refrain is being heard from respected companies such as Marketing Management Analytics, a marketing ROI measurement company, ACNielsen BASES and Ernst & Young. The latter put the failure rate of new U.S. consumer products at 95%. And as if that weren't enough, UCLA's Anderson School of Management found doubling advertising expenditures for established products increases sales just 1% to 2%. Advertisers aren't too overworked to advertise. They are afraid to fail.

We are all afraid to fail.

The same marketing industry that tries to keep this information out of the limelight also is oddly eager to shoulder the blame, proposing that the reason for all this mediocrity is just plain sloppy strategy, ineffective messaging, lack of targeting and a general need to refine the creative, the content and the media channels. All that is really needed, they suggest, is to go back and do what they have been doing poorly, and do it better.

I agree with them, in part – that is, we have absolutely been doing it poorly and can do it better. But, like my earlier customers that were not really prepared to leave the level they were on, neither is the marketing industry, as a whole, ready to shed its own dearly held mythology, that, like its customers, it believes is the Gospel Truth: Marketing can sell anything to anyone with the right message.

Here I must stand apart from most of my marketing peers, and strongly disagree. Marketing is a tool – a complex and many faceted tool – that involves what are commonly called the six P's: right product, people (customers,) placement, pricing, promotion and performance (of the product.) What we as marketers routinely overlook is the equal importance of product, people and performance, instead looking far more intently at placement, pricing and promotion. And oh, how we love promotion!

This is the precise reason why we have earned the snake oil salesman perception. We believe we have the power to sell the air itself to the masses, and make a profit in the process. As a matter of fact, we can, just as jumping can create the illusion of flight for a moment – but sooner or later, you will hit the ground. It just isn't sustainable.

The issue is there are too many companies and products that are pale copies of something else, and are also lacking in Purpose beyond a poorly defined quest for wealth and growth. There is nothing inherently bad about seeking

11

money. I personally am a huge fan of financial gain. There is also nothing to feel guilty about in growing a business venture. However, the world is both consciously and subconsciously seeking those products that improve their lives, and increasingly those that make society sustainable in the process, although currently society is still easily misled about what companies and products actually live up to this ideal, amid all the claims and noise.

Unfortunately, too many companies only give the idea of service to the greater good passing lip service, or worse, are intentionally abusing our society's health and resources, all in the interest of their own immediate gains. The companies giving lip service, we will call Prey Organizations, and the abusers, we will call Predator Organizations.

Prey Organizations tend to be scared, very alert to the movements of peers, trends, and competitors, They always are trying to move at breakneck speed, and stay ahead of the market, while doing more with less, because there is never enough. Their employees are frustrated and exhausted, and also tend to live in an anxious state most of the time. Make no mistake, however, these organizations can grow to enormous scale in this manner, and even endure for many decades by constantly accelerating, dodging and deflecting the proverbial bullet and beating the odds. It is the Prey Organization's employee morale which is the telling indicator behind the stripes of the organization, not its size or revenues.

Predator Organizations, on the other hand, while they also like to move fast, are far more focused on the deal, than generating tremendous public awareness. They tend to operate more behind the scenes, and their advertising and marketing is much more inspirational than product-centric. As I sat at the table a couple of decades ago with two mid-level executives from Siemens Energy and Automation, discussing an international conference they were hosting, one of them said in an off-handed way, "We (the energy industry) know almost to the day when fossil fuel will run out, and we have alternatives in place. But we are holding back on launching those because prices will go up before the resources run out." This statement is telling on a number of levels. First, the Predator psychology is shared throughout the management of the organization, and the focus is purely on money – regardless of any socio-enviro-economic impact. There also is a disassociation from what others experience as a result of their actions.

Other books address the idea of money, its power symbolism and the real power it holds in our psyche far more in depth than this book is intended to do. For now, I only discuss these two organizational personalities, since both the Prey and the Predator Organizations are swimming in a sea of sameness – and as marketers we are guilty of having been the silent 'yes men', which has made us appear disingenuous in the process. It is for this reason we, as marketers, are failing on an epic scale.

The Fools

"Throughout the centuries there were men who took first steps down new roads armed with nothing but their own vision. Their goals differed, but they all had this in common: that the step was first, the road new, the vision unborrowed, and the response they received—hatred. The great creators—the thinkers, the artists, the scientists, the inventors—stood alone against the men of their time. Every great new thought was opposed. Every great new invention was denounced. The first motor was considered foolish. The airplane was considered impossible. The power loom was considered vicious. Anesthesia was considered sinful. But the men of unborrowed vision went ahead. They fought, they suffered and they paid. But they won."

—AYN RAND, FOR THE NEW INTELLECTUAL

If you are going to grow, either at an organizational level or personal level, at some point you must become willing to run afoul of the opinions of others. It is a risk most of us only become ready for when we have become so uncomfortable wherever we currently are that we no longer care about the consequences of change, or we feel we are left no choice, because the alternative is equivalent to death. It is the rare individual who is willing to change with utter disregard of what others think – and I caution those of you reading this, who like myself delight in exploring new experiences and ideas: a cosmetic change purely for the sake of newness is not the type of change I am addressing. I am addressing the type of change that is so different that it makes you and those around you very uncomfortable – change like building a DeLorean, flying to the moon, the personal computer, hiring the first woman or African American CEO, inventing the airplane, the telephone, shutting down a division of a company that is over 50 years old and putting thousands of people out of work. Some of these ideas were wildly successful and others flopped miserably. The point is they all were panned by mass opinion.

This fear of the opinions of others is unfounded in reality, since their disapproval alone can cause us no physical harm, but the fear is deeply rooted in our social structure, since social rejection is tantamount to death in our unconscious mind. We go with the flow in order to ensure our safety in the group. The result is a cultural torpor where we mimic others in a profound lack of originality, creating stagnancy so deep, we are hardly aware of it.

Unlike Jonathan Gruber, MIT Professor and architect of Obamacare, I am not about to attack the general public as stupid. There is no doubt that culturally we are capable of mass stupidity – but I am making a sharp distinction between individual stupidity and mass stupidity. This is not a book for the masses. It is for the individual whose has that tickle in the back of your consciousness that says, *"Something isn't quite right here, although I cannot quite put my finger on it."* You are ready for a new idea. You are ready to become courageous and be true to your original nature.

Our culture is a macrocosm of the individual, and it learns by trial and error – through experiencing pain, disappointment, delight and abundance. The only way we can learn something is by experience and practice – otherwise it is only hearsay. Many marketers are experiencing frustration, even when they are "doing all the right things." These are the frontrunners, who are learning through their own experience and practice that, if nothing else, there has to be a better way.

This book is designed to help those same marketers, whether a CMO of an enterprise organization, or CEO of a start-up, develop the confidence to step outside the same-same thinking of the masses, and truly break through.

I will presume, if you are reading this book, you are not an intentional Predator Organization, as these organizations rarely experience marketing frustrations since their focus is so intently on the deal. If you suspect your organization or client might be one, however, you have your own soul work to do, and I wish you success in realizing that sooner or later (even decades later) your approach will ultimately eat *you* alive. It is not too late to escape this trap.

For those organizations that are timidly keeping with the pack of Prey Organizations, and thus lack clear individuated Purpose, other than to stay alive another day without being consumed, you have another option now, you were previously unaware of – become the Chimera Organization.

In Greek mythology, the Chimera was a monster – an abomination. It had the body of a goat, with the head of a lion and the tail in the form of a snake. This creature was, in fact, terrifying – even as a myth – to the people of the time, because they could not fathom an animal that was neither Predator nor Prey, and was utterly unique in its genetic composition. It was truly one-of-a-kind – which is, at a deep, often subconscious level, frightening to us all, because it implies any of us might be something other than we currently are. It implies somewhere beneath the surface we all are only barely hiding a terrifying monster of uniqueness that will scare away our fellows.

So, I invite you, if you dare, to enter the no man's land within your own creative source, and within your organization, to seek the uniqueness that is hidden there, that is too beneficial to us all to be Predator, and too powerful to be Prey.

Let's find your Chimera.

CHAPTER 2

Hunting the Chimera

"What a chimera then is man! What a novelty! What a monster, what chaos, what a contradiction, what a prodigy! Judge of all things, imbecile worm of the earth; depository of truth, a sink of uncertainty and error; the pride and refuse of the universe!"

— BLAISE PASCAL

A Chimera is something imaginary, which is hoped for ardently, but is, in fact, impossible. Still, as I referenced in the last chapter, many of our world's greatest achievements came about when an individual embraced what the majority had thought impossible previously. Impossible is just an idea – as is the Chimera. Our choice is: which idea we are going to embrace: limits or possibility?

Of course, this is all highly philosophical in nature, and it begs the question – how does any of this impact the marketing for Joe's BBQ? Whether Joe's is a line of seasonings and sauces, a single restaurant, or a national franchise, whoever is heading up marketing and advertising is looking to grow market share and build awareness. They have a sense of urgency and are looking, as I mentioned earlier, to take it to the next level or make a positive shift, like most clients who first walk in an agency's door. They don't have time to do theoretical soul searching about their unique Purpose and how they serve their community ("we support the local Food Bank!") They have done a brand audit, a focus group study, developed a mission and vision for their Team Members (no longer called employees) and allocated some solid advertising dollars in appropriate media.

So, with all that right action, we wonder, why is Joe's BBQ's key marketing stakeholder frustrated with results and reading this book? This scenario is repeated over and over again. An organization looks outside itself briefly when results don't match expectations, but when it is asked to question not only its tactics but also its strategy – and what's more – its original goals, and explore the possibility of whether poor results could come from a faulty or out-of-date starting point – the defenses go up immediately. The conversation ends with, "Just give us a price on a new campaign for the next quarter." The door to real change slams shut again. It happens all the time, as marketing guru, Seth Grodin says, "The trouble with working with a coach isn't that we don't know what to do. It's that we don't want to change our mind."

Question All Assumptions

*"Contrariwise,' continued Tweedledee, 'if it was so, it might be;
and if it were so, it would be; but as it isn't, it ain't.
That's logic."*

— LEWIS CARROLL, ALICE'S ADVENTURES IN WONDERLAND
& THROUGH THE LOOKING GLASS

Dr. Donald Sull, Senior Lecturer at the MIT Sloan School of
Management, and expert on strategy and execution in
turbulent markets, talks about "active inertia" within
organizations. This interesting phenomenon has seriously
injured some major companies who did not respond
effectively to changes in the marketplace. He references
once major players, such as Laura Ashley and Firestone,
whose brands continue, but have lost their momentum due to
changes in consumer preferences and economics.

In brief, Firestone had a strong company culture and was an
acknowledged industry leader – until Michelin hit the market
in the 60's with the radial tire. Firestone saw it coming, and
they too had a radial offering, but they were loath to close
their bias tire plants, and alter their production requirements
to match the new offering. Inertia – and decline – set in.

Laura Ashley was much the same. Once a strong brand that
embodied the romantic floral motif of an idealized British
countryside, it lost its allure as its female customer base
entered the workforce and chose corporate-friendly styles.
Seven CEOs later, the company still struggles with the

20

challenges of cost and efficiency in a style that has lost its luster. Inertia is killing it softly as one of its floral patterns.

Sull calls these companies out because they were, for a time, doing everything right, and when external shifts occurred, they did take action – but the actions they took were more of what they had been doing successfully initially, and not adaptive actions designed to meet the new landscape. They made some assumptions based on previous successes, and assumed more of the same would fix their struggles. The assumption was that to adapt to the landscape was to lose their core identity as company, and so they forged on, and lost tremendous market share in the process.

Despite the struggle of companies like Laura Ashley and Firestone, not all assumptions are destructive. Assumptions by their nature are neutral. The real challenge for companies occurs when they are, as an organization, unaware of the assumptions underlying their decisions. Unconscious assumptions are based on old, and often untested, ideas, which may or may not reflect the current reality. In fact, many companies are founded on unconscious assumptions, which can be severely limiting, if not life threatening, to the organization.

Assumptions are really a belief. After a very philosophical dinner with a client of mine, a while back, I had the opportunity to also entertain a conversation with his 19-yeaar-old son. After our dinner conversation about meaning and Purpose, my client wanted me to speak to his son, because, to his dismay, his son had espoused a nihilistic outlook upon entering college. Without any real introduction or ceremony, my client handed the phone to me with his son at the other end.

After some awkward hellos, I said to his son, "So, I understand you have decided you believe in nothing?"

The young man said, "Well, mostly nothing. I mean, I believe the sun will rise."

I agreed, "Yes. It's a safe bet. Nothing's guaranteed, of course. But as beliefs go, that one has good odds."

He laughed.
I added, "It's good to question beliefs of others, so you can determine what you believe for yourself."

I could almost see him nodding vigorously as he said, "Exactly!"

I added, "But you must believe in something."

"No," the son assured me, "I believe in nothing."

An idea came to me then, and I was talking less to the young man than to myself as I said, "Anything you believe in IS your belief. There can be no absence of belief. You cannot believe in nothing. Once you believe in it, it – even nothingness – is transformed into something –the thing which you believe in."

The young man said, "Let me think about that."

I expressed my thanks for the opportunity to explore ideas and we went our ways. But the interchange left a lingering tickle in my brain that what is true for individuals is true of organizations. I admired the young man for testing the boundaries of his own beliefs and the beliefs of others, which I suspect, when the initial questioning phase resolves itself, will make his own beliefs more definitive and unique to his personal experience.

If more organizations made it a standard operating procedure to regularly run an assumptions audit, just as many already run brand audits, they would see what assumptions lie beneath their current practices, examine how well they hold up to current reality, and then consciously decide whether to keep them or replace them with a new idea.

Assumptions are a tricky, slippery thing. They can go far back in memory – so far back that they are nearly invisible. Or they can be all tangled up in many very complex interlocked behaviors, that all hinge on the original assumption, the elimination of which would cause a great deal of stress, potential embarrassment, and even the "little death" of temporarily taking a step backward from the stated goal, in order to remove them initially. And that's just for the individual. It can be compounded 100-fold for an organization.

Typically, organizations that are operating in an unconscious assumption-rich environment use a number of similar catch-phrases that signal an audit is needed. These phrases sound like this:

- This is how we operate.
- It is important to the [CEO, President, Board, Leadership].
- We'll never get buy-in.
- We're doing everything right, but not getting the results you'd expect.
- The customers don't seem to understand what we have to offer.
- It's a tough market.
- We just can't seem to break through the noise.
- We need to get to market faster.
- We change slowly.
- Our training/hiring/on-boarding/morale/retention/sales/ production is not delivering results up to par.

All companies have basic assumptions, and most companies have an assumption problem. The scale of the problem is directly proportionate to the degree that the assumptions are unspoken, unconscious, unaddressed, and not in alignment with reality. The problem will not be hard to spot. It shows up in unmet expectations and frustration. It is almost as easy to address – once the stakeholders become willing to think differently. But be warned, new ideas are absolutely the most difficult thing to embrace.

If you look at each of the telling statements above, there is usually not one, but instead several, assumptions behind them – and not every assumption is necessarily out of alignment with reality. As an example, the first statement: "That's how we operate," is extremely broad. It could be addressing an operating model, or manufacturing process, or perhaps it is implying the industry functions in that manner and therefore so must the organization. Behind each of those ideas many assumptions were put into place initially to get to that decision to operate "that way."

Once an organization that has decided to do the challenging work of holding its assumptions up to the light of an audit, it needs to begin with the areas of frustration and underperformance, and gradually uncover the assumptions behind each process, one layer at a time. This is usually best accomplished with an outside facilitator, who does not have any emotional attachment to the processes themselves.

Depending on the scale and age of the organization, this process can take a tremendous amount of time – especially if it has never been done before. Essentially, an audit is a simple list, which has four excruciatingly challenging phases to it. Phase I requires a list what's frustrating or disappointing – it could be customer service response time or 4th quarter sales. There will initially be several, if not numerous, pain points. Particular categories such as sales or production can be on there several times for different reasons, in fact. However, this is not an exercise in granularity, so don't turn it into an exhaustive and exhausting attack on every nuance and detail that is wrong. That is not the point – and neither is finger pointing or blaming. It is bad form in an argument, and it is bad form here.

While an Assumption Audit should not get bogged down in the microscopic, it should be thorough. In brief, what should show up on Phase I is every (broad category) thing! If it is broken, get it out there. This is not strictly speaking, a marketing exercise. But everything your organization does, says, thinks, implies, believes and communicates in any way is ultimately a part of your marketing because it is your living brand. So, get in there and look at it!

Phase II is to briefly (five words or less) describe the issue. The word limit forces you and your team to be focused and precise. Thus, for each pain point there is a short comment about that particular item. For example, a Phase I pain point might be Trade Shows, and the Phase II descriptor might be "leads not visiting the booth". Go down the list, and add the descriptor in each area. It is relatively quick, and does not require overthinking. You know what's wrong. Just write it down. If your team disagrees, then there may be something more to it. If you aren't sure, keep moving. Either way, a pattern will emerge, and it is the pattern we are looking for.

Phase III is to then attach an impact to each descriptor. The impact is a word that describes what affect the pain is having on the organization. When you distill it down, there are really only five real potential impacts possible, and they are:

1.   Stability
2.   Integrity
3.   Growth
4.   Visibility
5.   Passion

For example, if you are not getting leads from your tradeshow presence, your descriptors would include Stability (there's a financial impact,) Growth (no new leads limits growth,) and Visibility.

Then in Phase IV it is time to look at the assumptions your organization has made in the impact areas in regards to the pain. Going back to our tradeshow presence example again, there are likely several assumptions, including that target customers are at not only the tradeshows you are participating in, but also you are assuming they are at tradeshows in the first place. You also are assuming you have the right staff and promotional team spearheading your tradeshow presence. Additionally, you are assuming your competitors are also there, and there is a "price of poker" investment for visibility. Add to that your assumptions that your messaging and promotion for the tradeshow is resonating with your targets.

But Phase IV actually asks you to go deeper than that. Phase IV asks you to examine not only the what, but the why. It is no longer about the tradeshow at all. Tradeshows are still a tactic. Go back. Look at what you are selling. Why are you selling it? What is your Purpose in the market that brought you here? What do you value? In other words, you will find that the tradeshow strategy is not the point at all.

Once you have an exhaustive list of assumptions around this pain point, it is time to test them. That's Phase V. Testing is the hardest part, for a number of reasons. The first reason is that many stakeholders have an emotional attachment to their assumptions – they really would prefer to only look at the tradeshow, not their beliefs about the company. Questioning them can not only make them wrong, it can also feel threatening to their job security in many cases.

The second reason stakeholders hate testing assumptions is it slows them down. Testing assumptions is generally a slow process. In the case of the tradeshow presence the process could be expedited by a survey of targets asking what tradeshows they attend and how regularly. Depending on how your target market responds, and how dedicated you are with funds and follow-through, you might get a statistically accurate set of data back. Yet, if you aren't even sure who you are as an organization (oh, I know you think you are, but we'll get to that) and what brought you here in the first place, that data is really pretty meaningless.

To explore the tradeshow attendee (and potential customers) further, you also can use anecdotal evidence, if you have enough of it. One of my clients, Temporary Accommodations, did this regularly, and in seven years, I rarely saw their anecdotal evidence prove inaccurate. In fact, their anecdotal evidence, which was based on speaking to customers at tradeshows and sales calls, was more accurate than most customer polls these days. The key is not to let one executive's opinion become the anecdotal evidence. That is addressing an assumption with another assumption, causing an infinite pain point loop that solves nothing.

A word of caution about what we will call the "substitution method" of posing another assumption to test a current assumption's validity. This is the most common course correction companies make, and it akin to swinging at a piñata, hoping to hit something. The companies recognize their tradeshow approach is failing, but instead of doing an assumption audit, they look around at other companies (interestingly, they often model on companies in categories completely unlike their own) and say, "They are having tremendous success at tradeshows! It looks to me like their staff are better trained. Let's train our staff better!" – and we're off to find a training partner for our tradeshow staff.

Meanwhile, no one has done any exploration of other assumptions or the validity of additional staff training against those other elements. This assumption swapping happens every day at companies of every size, shape and segment. As you probably have gathered by now, the results are highly unpredictable, and usually only mildly successful – for the most part because their Assumption Audit is no deeper than examining the tradeshow presence. If that's as deep as you go, don't bother, and for goodness sake, don't call it a true Audit.

If, however, an organization has done their Audit homework, and understands the five Phases of impact, when they find their tradeshow strategy is struggling, they can go back and look at their assumptions about Visibility, Stability and Growth. They ask themselves – do we know tradeshows really reflect what we stand for, and as a result are a place where we can connect with and close new customers? If we do, then we need to look at our approach, and audit our assumptions there. If we don't, then let's find out.

There's another important word of caution about the time component of these audits. What was true last year, five years, or fifteen years ago may not be true today. That is what tripped up both Laura Ashley and Firestone. Assumptions are fluid, dynamic things, requiring continuous examination, and adaptation. If they become rigid, your organization will stagnate. If you are not questioning assumptions regularly, they will rule you, and become rigidly entrenched before you even know it, and your Chimera becomes lost once more.

CHAPTER 3

You Are Not Your Customer

I'm starting with the man in the mirror
I'm asking him to change his ways
And no message could have been any clearer
If you wanna make the world a better place
Take a look at yourself, and then make a change.

— MICHAEL JACKSON, MAN IN THE MIRROR

At some point, every company assumes that what they would want is exactly what the customer wants – a seductively, and potentially disastrous idea that this very brief chapter will uncover and address. At a deep, universal level, those who identify themselves as their customer are right. We all want the same global things once our basic needs for food and shelter are met. Those things are: love and connection, comfort, variety, significance, growth, and to make a contribution. In those areas, we *are* all like our customers. However, how those needs and desires manifest individually are more like the unique nature of our fingerprints. This belief that we are – not are *like*, but actually *are* – our customer, denies the individuality of each customer, and is the organizational version of a married

32

couple assuming they can read each other's minds – with similarly devastating results.

The strong belief that we know our customers better than the customers know themselves can be fanatically held in some organizations. It typically has its origins with the founder, president, or CEO who has become too emotionally attached to the initial founding concept of the organization's offering. Most entrepreneurs build businesses to address a void they themselves felt in the marketplace. This gives them significance, and a deep sense of contribution, which they are loathe to let go of, even though the self-same void might be shifting right under their feet.

The originator of the attachment, if they have enough momentum and followers within an organization, can rapidly build an organizational culture where customers are told, instead of asked, what they need and want. When the customers then don't behave as predicted, the organization becomes irrationally frustrated, and develops a superior attitude to their unpredictable, "idiotic" customers. Customers are treated like short-sighted and ungrateful children, who are ultimately to be outwitted or overpowered. This is a far cry from answering a need in the marketplace. It is a far cry from the original vision.

Naturally, when a company has crossed into this adversarial mindset, the marketing materials will not tell customers the company's true opinion of them, but the customers know. In every interaction, the organization presents its beliefs. Delta Airlines is an excellent example of this – and how to change the dynamic almost overnight. The airline's "big dog" approach in the 1990's and early 2000's eventually sent it into bankruptcy. During that time period it had the most flights in many hubs, and charged accordingly, but had a horrible record of on-time departures, and treated customers with only cursory interactions. The customers standing in the queue (of which I was one) were frustrated, dis-enfranchised, and felt as though they really had little choice or voice.

Then post-bankruptcy things changed dramatically. Every flight a customer takes they receive a survey which you can see what the airline is placing value on – the customer experience and interaction – and the results show in how the employees treat the customers. The in-flight safety videos became a highlight of the flight, and if premium legroom is what you value, then it became available too. If something is malfunctioning at your seat – the audio, the tray, the internet – you can expect rewards point to be added to your Skymiles account, if you have one.

Delta is not a low-cost provider, but neither does it try to be. It is one of a handful of premium airlines, and it acts like one now with attentiveness and service those premium travelers recognize and respect.

Regardless of how recently an organization was founded, it is easy to lose touch with customers' true needs and desires very rapidly, just by becoming absorbed in new initiatives and growth strategies. Most company's claim that the customer is at the center of every decision they make. Yet to sit in the room where those precise decisions are being discussed is to see that this is actually only rarely the case. As often as not, the focus is on shareholder or corporate issues, and not on customers at all, other than as a numeric quantity to be managed like pawns on the chessboard.

I assure you, a chorus of voices is now crying out that I am mistaken, and how could I possibly say such a thing? Yet I have seen it too often. So have most of you. The external and internal pressures can feel too great to ignore. The revenue becomes more important than anything else, and it is growth at all costs.

I am not suggesting that you should ignore those pressures. I am only suggesting that *if* the customer becomes your organization's *primary* focus, not just in theory, but in practice, then the internal and external pressures become easier to solve. Richard Branson is quoted as saying, "The way you treat your employees is the way they will treat your customers." He's not putting employees' above customers' needs. He is identifying that you cannot diminish one for the other. If anyone understands that they would have no employees at all – nor any company – without their customers – it is Richard Branson.

There are many books about how to stay in touch with your customers and how to ensure you keep an open line of communication between you. There also are legendary stories about how insights gained from customer feedback transformed the success of numerous companies. To rehash that is not my Purpose here. My focus is only to point out that if you are convinced you have your finger on the pulse of your customers every wish, but they are not buying like you expect, then you likely have a disconnect, and until you explore that, no amount of marketing will solve any gaps in your understanding of what your customers want.

CHAPTER 4

Hello, Ego!

The ultimate aim of the ego is not to see something, but to be something. "

— MUHAMMED IQBAL

We all have egos. It is the part of our consciousness that encompasses our sense of self-esteem, self-worth, self-importance, self-respect, self-reliance and self-confidence. Those who have risen to leadership within organizations tend to have greater sense of those attributes by virtue of their power within the system. There is nothing inherently wrong or bad about that. Where the ego goes awry is when the sense of self-worth and other self-centric awareness are not actually in a balanced alignment with reality, because the ego has another function, which is to mediate between the conscious and the unconscious part of our mind, making it responsible for reality testing.

When the ego gets confused is when we have lost our perspective on reality. Then our ego will drive decisions, and those decisions are always made out of emotional attachment and a deep neediness to regain some sense of self-centricity. The irony is that we humans are operating as purely emotional beings, while pretending we are doing nothing of the sort. In short, decisions will be fear-based, while we insist they are as rational at their core.

In marketing terms, this manifests as an unfounded, unilateral decision to place an ad or sponsorship without the backing of foundational information necessary to validate the desired benefit will be generated. Often company morale is cited, or a belief that this visibility has worked for others and so it must work for them, or they have seen others like their company there, and so on. I have been a witness to these decisions more times than I care to count. My personal favorite is, "I know I would buy based on this!" (Which goes back to You Are Not your Customer in the last chapter.)

As an example, a technology company with only about $10,000 to spend on an entire marketing campaign for a new product offering targeted to a specific type of airline was spearheaded by an executive who could not let go of the idea that had captured his imagination, of having a billboard right outside the largest of those carriers' headquarters.

Now, that idea is neither a good idea nor a bad idea taken in isolation. However, billboards, especially in the location he wanted, were non-existent. Therefore, billboards would have to be purchased on multiple entry highway arteries. Each billboard would cost $3,000-$5,000 per month. This left no budget for any other materials or outreach.

The previous example is not a judgment on whether the decision to utilize billboard placement was correct or not. It might have been the perfect solution. The real problem was the manner in which the decision was being made. From its inception, it was purely an emotional choice, without any back up information of relevance. That's not to say that a wealth of highly intelligent rationale wasn't being used too justify the decision! The reasons ranged from the inability to reach the key decision makers through other avenues such as email, phone and mail, combined with the high visibility of these billboards.

Rationale, by definition is simply a set of reasons or a logical basis for a course of action. What we like to forget is that we can rationalize our way into just about any action we are inclined to pursue – especially if we are extremely intelligent. Reasons exist in abundance. That doesn't guarantee they will deliver the results one might hope. Along with this lack of certainty come the frustration and disassociation of the rest of the team, who are entirely aware of the arbitrary nature of the initiative. The team had their own opinions (discussed surreptitiously in the hallways, instead of collaboratively in front of the decision-maker who clearly had already decided) such as how the previous business had been won through relationship-building, which billboards could never deliver, and the purchase of a list of contacts cost roughly the same as the billboards, with the opportunity for the sales team to then pursue the relationships directly. Additionally, the elephant in the room for everyone was that only one customer was the focus, and none of the other carriers even factored into the equation.

In the end, the billboards didn't happen because executives at an even higher level vetoed the plan. The campaign involved some whitepapers and a presentation with a nominal list purchase. Interestingly, the results were poor, and eventually the product was discontinued. So the question presents itself – was the billboard idea so bad after all? Would it have yielded better results? Was the product truly addressing the needs of customers? Or was there a deeper process issue within the company that obstructed the sales team's efforts? So many questions arise out of failures – ones that could and should have been asked at the inception rather than in post mortem.

Regardless, here is the fundamental question – How do we know when the decision is based on fear rather than reality? I find while the answer is in the results, we don't have the luxury of such guesswork. We must learn, and learn true reasoning, through a variety of means, before we begin practicing our theories in the lab of real-world business.

Marketing, like the business it serves, is measured against its results – predictable, repeatable results. Results happen when you have identified a need and a solution; build awareness of the solution to a reasonable target population for momentum, and deliver the appropriate value associated with the need. The challenge here is that there are three critical components to that results equation that are highly variable, and (here's my controversial statement) *often nearly impossible to accurately measure*. They are:

1. Confirmation of precise need
2. Location and frequency for optimal awareness
3. The value proposition

Add to that list a fixed budget that will never seem large enough, and businesses start getting very reactionary instead of responsive. Because the three components are so difficult to pin down into a predictable pattern of cause and effect, many marketers believe they might as well just make an educated guess, because the results seem the have about the same ratio of success.

Before I go any further, let's dig a little deeper into that statement I just made about the extreme difficulty around getting firm intelligence on market needs, location for placement and the right value proposition. There are a tremendous number of tools available in just about any price point to help gain clarity on those questions. There are excellent companies that can perform consumer surveys, get feedback, provide industry research, forecast trends, and so on. They absolutely are worthwhile, and can help shape a company's strategy quite dramatically and with great effectiveness. I often recommend this approach early on with my clients to confirm what they actually do and don't know. Typically, if they have not implemented some sot of customer polling, they will find out at least one very substantial piece of information that shifts their approach.

One such example was a human resources software company that held an annual user conference that always got strong marks from those who attended every year. The company was polling the 30% of customers who were attending regularly, listening to their input and adjusting accordingly. However, they we not polling customers (whose contact info they already had) who were *not* attending, in order to better understand why they were absent. Additionally, their goal was to have at least 70% of customers participating every other year at a minimum, and found themselves unable to make any headway in growing the event, which represented their largest single marketing initiative for customer retention and expansion.

At our recommendation, the company allowed us to poll both attendees and non-attendees with a brief survey, and what we found shocked them into a drastic shift in their process. We discovered that 80% of non-attendees had never heard of the conference! Their main source of information was their sale representative, and the reps were not communicating about the conference. To shift this behavior, a sales incentive was put in place for the most increase in customers at the conference. The result was a 50% lift in attendance at the next event.

Another example of the power of customer surveys comes from a meeting industry organization that was finding its membership numbers dropping in the double-digits annually. The organization's goal was to appeal to both buyers and suppliers, and it promised an equal distribution of the two member categories. What they were finding is that suppliers showed up at events to network with buyers, but they were showing up in larger numbers while buyers were staying away because they didn't want to be hounded by the suppliers.

The events were a huge revenue generator for the organization that had positioned itself as a leading education provider for buyers in the region. The answer, the organization had decided in a committee without benefit of anything more than anecdotal insight from younger, non-buyers was to generate a social media blitz using Facebook, LinkedIn and Twitter.

When my agency was engaged to help re-brand the organization, the first thing we did was to develop a survey for buyers. One of the key insights was that they were rarely on social media. Social media was not the way to reach them. The other key piece of information was that they felt the content was too rudimentary and the number of suppliers was too overpowering. Within a few months we had developed a marketing message, event content strategy as well as website, and other initiatives such as sponsored webcasts and whitepapers to elevate buyer involvement without over-saturation from suppliers, and still generating revenue for the association. The organization embraced most of what was suggested, and then within a year, went right back to what it had been doing, and the numbers continued to drop.

Why did they stop short of the finish line? Why did they spend all this money and then pull back? The answer is that they are a volunteer-staffed organization, and the leadership changes every year. Each new Board has an agenda that it wants to push forward to grow personal brands under the auspices of the organization's brand. The hand-off between presidents is wildly variable, and the personalities become the driver, not a consistent brand or Purpose. Sound like any political system you can think of off-hand?

In short, the information that is required for realistic and informed decisions making (Need, Awareness, Value) is hard to come by, but when it is identified, it is only occasionally acted upon, and event then, with poor consistency.

Here comes the kicker – organizations which do push out surveys and customer polls often do so with an agenda attached. They ask leading questions that guide their respondents to provide the answers they want! Here's what a leading question looks like:

Q: What is the most beneficial aspect of Product X?
     A: Features
     B: Functionality
     C: Expansion Options
     D: Accessibility
     E: Other: _____

Here's a non-leading version of the same question:
Q: Do you find Product X beneficial? Y/N
Q Part B: If so, in what way?
Q Part C: If not, why not?

The difference is enormous. The first question assumes the product benefits the recipient. In the second, the idea that it may not meet a need is at least willing to be entertained. It also allows the recipient to provide a more open-ended response that is personal and therefore more insightful.

Companies invest enormous resources to development of new product, features and functions assuming they are what the customers need and want. To find out, after the fact, that this is not the case, can mean someone loses their job or an entire department is eliminated. This has a tendency to generate a lot of fear, which in turn creates – often unconsciously – un-balanced market research.

Things become even more convoluted when someone whose job is on the line hires a marketing or research firm. The person doing the research and the firm supporting the research are far from "disinterested". They are *deeply* interested in proving the validity of their product or offering regardless of the truth. This is the real world. Even though it is the world in which marketing operates, this approach need not be a given.

If your marketing initiatives are currently struggling to demonstrate measurable results, or results that align with expectations, then before you decide what needs to be adjusted in the messaging, and before you settle on what channels need to be developed, look at what assumptions are being made, and whose agenda has been leading the charge. Once again, this is nearly impossible to undertake this investigation solely on an internal basis. People's livelihoods are riding on the answers – or, at least, that's what they believe. Fear is driving the train. Egos are absolutely in the way. The irony is that if executives were really willing to be transparent both with their objectives and their fears, the possibility of finding a real solution would be so much easier and intensely more likely. Instead, sadly, the game of cloak and dagger with the truth remains the rule, not the exception, and companies stay stuck.

CHAPTER 5

Finding Your Purpose

"My dear family, guess what? Today I found out what my special Purpose is for. Gosh, what a great time I had. I wish the whole family could've been here with me. Maybe some other time, as I intend to do this a lot. Every chance I get."

— THE JERK

In the previous chapter we stripped away a lot of the underbrush that grows up over time and covers up the original Purpose of an organization. We set out to uncover the powerful uniqueness of your organization that, when identified, will shine like a beacon for every strategic marketing decision that needs to be made. We can ask ourselves: Is this in alignment with our unique Purpose? Then let us proceed. Is it out of alignment? Then let us find a better solution, which is to find our Purpose.

Finding the organization's Purpose is what it means to find your true differentiator. It is to find your Chimera. To reiterate, it is not better customer service, innovation for innovation's sake, superior quality, faster response times, more expert staff, greater resources, or 24/7 availability – although each of those things can support it, they are strengths. They are tools in the toolkit.

Most companies are aware of the importance of "key differentiators" to their marketing success, but they confuse what that really means badly. They make strength statements, and provide a list of their strengths to their sales teams. They proudly refer to their strengths as differentiators. They are not.

Here is the hierarchy of terms and how they build on each other – and we as marketers are guilty of confusing them as often as our clients are:

1. Purpose – The unique reason that your company exists and creates meaning for both employees and customers alike.

2. Differentiators - in 1933 Edward Chamberlin proposed the concept of differentiators in his *Theory of Monoplastic Competition*. They are defined as the business attribute(s) and/or unique value that clearly separate it from the competition in a particular marketplace. In principle these differentiators must be unique, measurable and defendable. We addressed a number of attributes companies tend to refer to as their unique differentiators back on page 4. Those items so

commonly called differentiators are actual core strengths.

3. Core Strengths – these are what an organization is really consistently excellent at doing. They support the differentiators, which, ideally arise from the organization's Purpose.

What happens more often, however, is the order of first identifying a Purpose, which then is responsible for creating differentiators, which finally leads to a solid set of core strengths, is actually reversed. The business model is founded on a leader's (or leaders') core competencies, not a driving Purpose.

Let me give you an example: When I started my first agency in 1997, The WOW Factory, I did so based on my core competency at the time, graphic design. The company I worked for prior to WOW was imploding, and I needed a job. I was ready to work for myself, and so I created my own company – with one employee – me! My core competencies were a strong work ethic, great attention to detail, highly accessible, responsive, and relatively cost-effective. While I like to congratulate myself for being a rather creative individual, my creativity was not a strength, because I was too bogged down in high-stress deadlines and taking on too much low-paying work right out of the gate.

It was not until I was well established, with four employees before I really saw myself as actually competing for business. This was an idea that came from my first VP of Sales who began looking for talking points. It was at that time, about two years into the company that we began to talk in terms of differentiation. Our differentiators were developed by default, as we looked at ourselves in the mirror and said, "Hmmm. How are we different from *them* in a way that addresses a customer need?" The answer we settled on was that we were a small, cost-effective boutique agency that was capable of big agency creative (capable, yes – actually doing it – not so much) without big agency pricing. So, not surprisingly, what we became – and stayed – for the duration of the WOW Factory was an agency that found itself always competing on price to such a degree that it became a conflict within the organization, as project managers were increasingly demanded to do more with less budget and not erode margins. Our focus became on the dollars, even though we gave lip-service to creative and innovation.

When it came time to create the then inescapable mission/vision statements (remember, this was the early 2000's, please) we again, backed into it. At this point the executive team was inextricably committed to the company, which was our source of livelihood. We were terrified to try and reinvent something. Instead we had to re-dress what we had created. Candidly, not even I can remember those early mission statements. They were meaningless.

This very same backwards approach is, I believe, a large part of the reason why most companies turn up their noses at mission statements today, saying they are meaningless. Of course they are! We are slapping them on top of reality, not generating reality from them. And that is a meaningless endeavor. What's worse, it is dishonest.

I am convinced, through volumes of conversations with others over the past 25 years, that my own personal experience as a beginning entrepreneur is the unfortunate norm, not the exception. I have heard the same story over and over and over again from healthcare companies, staffing companies, manufacturing companies, technology companies, retail companies, and on and on. No industry is immune to this Primary, Creative Thought at the company's inception: "I/We can do this as well or better than anyone. So why not go for it?"

The other, accompanying thought is, "Besides, my/our other option is to go do this for someone else, and we've already done that. I think I can make more money this way, doing what I already know." We will call this accompanying thought the Second Thought. It kind of sucks a little joy out of the Primary, Creative Thought, bringing it back to "reality", doesn't it?

I know the common nature of this thought process, because I've had it myself, and discussed it with far too many founders to believe it's a rarity. However, what I also know is that there is another, currently rarer thought process that instead says, "I believe my experience has taught me enough to break away from what I have known and address this need of X, which I recognize as unmet. I am uniquely qualified to change this current state of affairs."

We will call this accompanying thought, which can occasionally appear instead of Second Thought, the Disruptive Thought. So, Second Thought takes the Primary, Creative Thought that says, "I'm great at this, and I'm going for it," and immediately diminishes it back to status quo with "doing what I already know." Second Thought is actually a very fearful and reactive thought in response to the Primary, Creative Thought. Second Thought, let's play it pretty safe, shall we?

On the other hand, Disruptive Thought takes the Primary Creative Thought and not only supports it, it even ups the ante. Disruptive Thought piles on with, "Not only am I going for it – I'm going to take this somewhere not yet dreamed of!"

This thought process happens, often unheard, in the head of the individuals responsible for the company. So what if you are not one of them? What if you work for a company that has been around for years, or decades, and you suspect – or are absolutely convinced – that your organization is operating solely on Second Thought, and not Disruptive Thought? Is it too late? Are you doomed to a professional life operating in a good place, but not great place, and often filled with frustration around your marketing traction? Of course not! That would be the end of this book, if it were.

Most companies begin with Second Thought, and most never make it to Disruptive Thought. Disruptive Thought – the game changer – becomes a much more frightening proposition the longer a company is in business without it. The longer a company exists, in whatever level of success it experiences, the harder it is to shift its focus, for fear of losing whatever traction (processes, messaging, existing customers, investments) it has. The reflexive solution in Second Thought organizations is to do just more of Second Thought: which included second guessing, blaming, re-organizing, etc. – and they keep on trying the same actions with greater intensity, because Disruptive Thought implies changing the status quo – which is the default reason for a Second Thought organization's being.

What I am describing is the Purpose Paradox – to find your Purpose, you only need to go back to the original idea – the idea that I have the ability to do this (whatever "this" may be) better. Then, instead of focusing on *what* (for ourselves, and to make more money) and look instead at the *why* (to fill the unmet need.) The This frustrating and limiting Purpose Paradox originates in the assumption that to rediscover to the Primary, Creative idea is to go backwards. The truth is that uncovering the Primary, Creative Idea reignites the organizational spark. The Primary, Creative

Idea is pure and simple. It is the source of an organization's creative energy, and it is renewed by the same fire of original passion.

At this point I need to stop for a moment and make a very important statement about an underlying assumption: Money (earnings, revenue, profit) is *never* your Purpose. It can be, and usually is, the *result* of pursuing your Purpose, since when you fill a need, people will pay you – often handsomely – for your unique solution. However, when you make purely financial gain your Purpose, not only do you become a Predator, you have created the least fulfilling, and most stressful, environment for yourself and your employees.

I know many (most notably my first VP of Sales) who would aggressively argue about the rightful place of money. They would likely accuse me of being unrealistic at best, and subversive at worst. In response, I have only this to say – I personally am a big fan of money. I really, truly appreciate it, and everything it can and does provide me – comfort, pleasure, safety, power and freedom. I am not proposing we work solely for the pleasure of our passions, setting aside all material wealth. Instead, I am suggesting we have habitually placed money in the wrong location in the hierarchy of building a successful, satisfying business. Money is not the starting point. Money is a by-product of abundance consciousness which is to be cultivated in *all* its forms.

The prevailing wisdom among organizations is that profit, size and market share are the measuring stick of success. The larger they are and the more profit they generate, the better they are assumed to be, and by association, the more effective their marketing, their strategy, and their initial vision. My stance is that scale and earnings are worthwhile measurements, but that they are not the only ones, and sometimes, when they are viewed in isolation, they are misleading.

Just as a balloon can be overfilled with air to the point of bursting, a company can grow beyond a sustainable point. It either explodes or it implodes. The reasons are wildly varied, from poor ethics of Enron, to market evolution that outstripped the initial need, such as Woolworth's. There are scores of books on this subject as well, which makes it all the more curious why so many people still stubbornly believe money and size are the sole proof of success.

Fulfillment of the basic human need for meaning is another measurement for an organization's success. It is a measurement that is rarely used, and when it is, lacks consistency in how it is measured. What we are talking about is a driver of both employee morale and customer loyalty. This is usually measured via a standard satisfaction survey, which only hints at the core issue of meaning, and only scratches the surface with perceived value, which is not the same thing at all.

If a company understands its Purpose, then it will communicate it, and it will check in with its people to assess how well it is delivering on that Purpose regularly. An inescapable example of such a company is Apple. Its Purpose, from the outset, was to make computers personally accessible and friendly. There was a time when it drifted off Purpose, but it returned to it with iTunes, and has continued to build its following, not just among the creative set, but globally. With the demise of Steve Jobs, Apple is at a turning point. Can it maintain its initial uniqueness, or will it sink into sameness?

There are those who would argue that Apple has begun to drift again, focusing on competing with Samsung and other technology companies rather than keeping its eye internally on its own Purpose. Only time will tell if this is the case.

Honda developed the Purpose to "be the company the world wants to exist". The problem with that Purpose is it is too all encompassing, and therefore unapproachable by both employees and consumers (if they knew about it.) Not that this Purpose has stopped its growth or its financial standing. What I am proposing is that a lack of clear Purpose leaves a company exposed and vulnerable to another competitor who does exactly what they do – only faster, or cheaper, or more conveniently.

Apple, if it continues to stay on Purpose, will continue looking for new, innovative and better ways to make computer technology more personal and friendlier with each product in its portfolio. Ironically, this makes Apple more likely to be voted "company the world wants to exist" in a corporate popularity contest today, than Honda. Why? Because it fills a unique need and has a clarity about its own Purpose.

If You Don't Know Where You're Going, Any Road Will Do

Organizations are typically as confused about how to determine their Purpose as they are about defining their key differentiators. To articulate the Purpose, a company must understand what a Purpose really looks like. Here are several attributes of a true organizational Purpose:

1. It is specific to what the company provides in the way of goods and services
2. It is focused on the customer's actual needs
3. It is aspirational

My most-recent agency existed to demystify and make effective marketing accessible to companies of all sizes. We focus on business to business organizations, primarily, but that's secondary to our Purpose, and so, if a consumer organization needs our unique skill set, we look at that request, and ask ourselves, is this off-Purpose for us? Sometimes it actually is. But that doesn't mean it always is. Ours is not a mission statement. It is not a vision statement. It is a statement, quite simply, about what we do. We are not describing how we do it, how much money we are making from it, or even saying the typical "for ourselves, for our customers and for our partners/shareholders". In a Purpose statement, all that inclusion is unnecessary. It assumes that whoever is involved, and whomever is served, is participating in, supportive of, and benefiting from our company's Purpose.

Here's the critical component that it took me years to understand: Our unique Purpose is not about staking an original claim. We are not inventing what has never seen the light of day necessarily. It is a rare organization that could ever claim that distinction. Instead we are claiming an original approach.

Apple is about making the personal computer more personal, but they are not the only ones to ever attempt that. Starbucks did not invent the idea of the coffee shop as a community hangout. The Wright Brothers were not the first ones to attempt to fly. No best-selling author has a lock on the format of their novel. Where the originality exists is in the process and approach.

Where it gets muddy, confusing and noisy is that too many organizations tweak the approach only ever so slightly, and then call that original. When widgets have been made out of iron for an eternity, and along comes a company that makes them out of bronze, they can become known for their unique materials and style. However, any other widget maker can come along and make bronze widgets too. If the same company comes along and creates a widget that eliminates a step in the assembly process of other thingamajigs then that is original, and will alter the entire process. A need has been filled.

But let me be very clear on this point – the company that eliminated the step in the assembly process can not claim that better widget manufacturing is their Purpose. They hopefully have a Purpose that says something about improving assembly processes everywhere. If they do, then when company X comes along and emulates their one-step widget (and they *will*) then our widget company will already be on to their next process improvement ideas – because that's what they do. It's their Purpose. It is what they are known for.

Some readers may wonder why the bronze widget is not enough of a Purpose. First of all, the product is never the Purpose. The product arises from the Purpose. That said, bronze might be the outcome of the widget company's Purpose, if bronze altered the customer's own experience or approach. Perhaps bronze widgets are better conductors, and so the thingamajig actually operates faster and

efficiently. This might be in alignment with a Purpose to "improve assembly processes of thingamajigs everywhere".
So if you work at one of those companies that isn't operating with a specific, focused, aspirational Purpose, then you need to find one for the sake of your brand, your marketing, your longevity, your morale, and your ability to compete effectively over time. The unfortunate truth is that this critical component to inside-out marketing cannot be initiated anywhere other than in the leadership. If an organization is a holocracy (managementless, led by the employees,) like Patagonia, then they have no further to look than in the mirror. Interestingly, however, holocracies seem to almost universally already have a Purpose. By in large, it is typically the entrenched, hierarchical organizations, and the contrastingly fast-growth, entrepreneurial start-up organizations that find themselves floundering in the Purposeless quicksand of assumptions.

Taking time to reflect, much less embracing the idea the organization might need to take a step back to its origins, feels like organizational suicide. It is a paradox, that the very thing that terrifies management might save the organization in the end. Perhaps this book can help organizations take a deeper look into their reasons, and find the willingness to "risk it all" in order to grow it. It is possible to do – in sweeping moves, but also in gradual evolution. A starting point can be as easy as conversations around what needs your organization addresses uniquely in its market, and how it might continue to address them in ever more innovative ways.

Then, begin to articulate these discoveries everywhere you can, both internally and externally. Start by placing the largest portion of your resources and your intentions directly on these initiatives you uncover. Let others know what you are doing. Enlist them in the shift, but don't wait on them to take action. You are the one with the vision. Lead from wherever you live within the organization. Like a white blood cell within the body of the organization, you can create noticeable healing from the inside out. Your actions need not be at the sacrifice of someone else's sacred cow either. Let it be an addition if necessary initially. All it takes is incremental action to begin to see a change.

You can do this at any time. If not now, when?

CHAPTER 6

The Problem with Life

"Life! Don't talk to me about life! Brain the size of a planet, and what do they ask me to do? Open doors!"

— MARVIN,
THE MANICALLY DEPRESSED ROBOT,
HITCHIKERS GUIDE TO THE GALAXY

The problem with life is that it is unpredictable and frequently does not operate according to our best-laid plans. It is full of people! And circumstances! This is no less true in business than it is in our personal affairs. It tugs and pulls at our resolve, and challenges what we feel to be true, right and important.

Like Marvin, the Manically Depressed Robot from Douglas Adams' *Hitchhikers Guide to the Galaxy*, we are constantly barraged with other people's (mostly bosses and customers) demands that we drop what we are doing proactively and react to their urgent needs. There are times when reacting is right – and there are times when it is not. Knowing the difference is what keeps you and your organization on Purpose, even in a culture that is operating with very little

Purpose, wallowing instead in a wealth of crisis. The direct correlation that exists between the level of Purpose and the level of serenity in any organization is no accident – and the difference in approach is clear between Purpose-driven *respo*nse and frustrating, stress-inducing *reaction*.

Purpose creates a proactive process that operates at a higher level of effectiveness. Purpose-driven companies have few day-to-day crises, and when they do, the crisis is dealt with quickly and smoothly, while assumption-infested organizations seem to leap from one crisis to the next with very little margin for error.

I don't think I exaggerate much when I state that just about every business coach is championing the best way to de-stress your work life in order to de-stress your whole life, so you can then focus on what's fulfilling. Stress-free generally equates to utopia for most of us (and yes, we are aiming very low in that regard.) Crisis-free generally equates to stress-free, whether it is a time crisis, financial crisis, self-esteem crisis, health crisis, family crisis, political crisis, social crisis, or crisis of faith – and whether it is personal, local, national or global. Conversely, crisis equates to stress, and when we are less stressed, we perceive fewer crisis. This is an infinite loop no matter which angle you look at it from. Yet most companies operate somewhere in the yellow to orange range of crisis at all times, if we are to compare it to our Homeland Security safety rankings, with an occasional dip into the red zone of high alert status, which can make yellow and orange seem mild by comparison.

Business effectiveness and efficiency experts of a wealth of tools to help us navigate the choppy waters of life, and most of the tools work to some degree. (One might argue they work to the degree with which they are actually applied.) However, I have tried a handful myself over the years, and while some really were transformative, others tended to make me more manic, by asking me to operate faster and more on the surface, rather than within my deeper more intuitive, authentic self. Regardless, until I stopped to assess my Purpose – both in life and in my work – I remained a leaf in the wind of others demands.

All the amazing tools in the world will not provide you, nor your organization, a Purpose. No Getting Things Done, Keirsey Temperament Sorter, Habits of Highly Effective People, SMART Goals, or Lean Management Structure will uncover your assumptions, move you from Secondary Thought to Disruptive Thought, nor guide you to your ultimate goal. They all assume you have done that work already and that you are operating consciously towards an objective that is sound. So it is little wonder that people (and the companies they create) follow these business efficiency fads much like we personally follow diet fads, picking them up with all the hope in the world that they will transform us, and then letting them slide sooner or later, in some level of frustration or complacency. At a surface level we desperately want to believe these solutions work, while at a deeper level, we are convinced the peace and order we are seeking is a non-existent fairytale.

Life happens. No organizational, process or efficiency model will change that. Markets fluctuate, economies crash, CEOs misbehave (or worse,) competitors advance, hostile takeovers blindside us, production struggles, reorganizations dampen morale, key employees leave to start a competing company or suffer a catastrophic illness, sales falter, customers can't seem to decide until the last minute, and on and on. How you handle your daily email flow is secondary in the face of these pressures.

However, a Purpose is a game changer when life happens. It doesn't change what happens at all. What it does do is change how you and your company *experience* it! It transforms your reaction into a considered response. It removes fear and replaces it with both acceptance and appropriate action.

Facing a hostile takeover? Let's go back to our Purpose. Our Purpose is to make personal computers more personal. Will the takeover affect this Purpose? If yes, then we need another option, and will explore those, even if it is to ride it out until we can go elsewhere and recommit to our Purpose. If no, then the vehicle for executing our Purpose is irrelevant. Either way, all the other noise, fear, confusion, and anxiety is avoided or at least minimized. So is the stress.

A company's marketing is a reflection of its corporate culture. If it is fearful, the result will be frequent changes in messaging, approach and channel use over a very short period of time. Many companies are in denial that they are fear-based, so to help you determine if you organization is, here are the alternate phrases that are code phrases for fear:

1. We operate under a lot of pressure.
2. He/she/they are on my case about this.
3. I have to get everyone's buy-in.
4. It's very political.
5. We have to act now, or lose this opportunity.
6. How are we going to explain this?
7. I know it doesn't make any sense, but it's just how we do it. (Don't ask.)
8. He'll/She'll never go for that.
9. There's a lot of tension about this.
10. They just decided on X, and they need it now.
11. Mr./Ms. Executive finally chose to pay attention and now we have to change everything.

These are only examples of the types of telltale phrases that belie systemic organizational fear. If one person uses them, or they are only used in regards to a single individual, that dynamic will resolve itself quickly within a fearless organization. Yet, it is rare to find an organization where one of these phrases is used that the others are not also present in abundance. The list can be endless but they all involve reaction to others, bitterness, frustration, urgency, defeatism and often, cynicism. These are the phrases that also signal a loss or lack of Purpose within the organization. The focus is squarely on the relational dynamics and just as squarely absent from any sense of Purpose or meaning to what is being done within the organization on a daily basis.

To drive the difference home, here are the opposite phrases to each listed above, which can be heard in organizations that, for the most part, are acting out of Purpose, not fear:

1. We operate at a fast pace.
2. He/she/they are eager to see the outcome.
3. I am empowered to bring solutions to the group.
4. It's a collaborative environment.
5. Now would seem like the best time, if we can do it effectively.
6. Let me see if I understand what happened, and how we can correct this.
7. I know we are open to fresh approaches, if they make sense.
8. We might find him/her resistant to that, but what are the pros and cons?
9. This is of primary importance to the team.
10. New information has come to light and we should look at a redirect.

11. Mr./Mrs. Executive had some questions about our approach which we should address before we proceed.

These phrases are solution-focused, proactive, positive, energetic, and dynamically open to the possibility that things can and do change. However, these individuals see themselves as architects of the change, rather than victims of it. So, in Purpose-driven organization when markets do fluctuate, economies do crash, CEOs do misbehave, competitors do advance, hostile takeovers do blindside us, production does struggle, reorganizations do dampen morale, key employees do leave to start a competing company, sales do falter, customers can't seem to decide until the last minute, and on and on, our Purpose-driven company's employees, while not unaffected, are also not sent spinning into a meltdown. In fact, they are far more resilient, and already schooled in looking for the solution, rather than rolling in the muck.

What this means is that their marketing is aligned with their culture's vision. It stays above the fray. When Starbucks launched its red, holiday (as opposed to red, *Christmas*) cup, and received loud criticism for pandering to political correctness and not taking a strong stance as pro-Christmas, the company remained mute. They continued to present their red cups full of their trademark multi-syllabic, hot beverages, during the entire holiday season, and allowed the defenders and the critics to have their arguments, mostly on social media. It was irrelevant to their Purpose. When the holiday season was over, they went back to their regular cups and continued selling hot, multi-syllabic beverages, in keeping with their Purpose, and despite the unexpected onslaught life had just thrown at them.

A company or an individual that is able to look inward, know their truth, independent of what is swirling about them, will make greater headway with only mild stress. Decisions will be easier. Focus will be clearer. Employees will be happier and more productive. Marketing will be more compelling and resonant. Growth will be steady and strong. This is assuming, of course, Purpose is bigger than market trends, and this flexible and dynamic. Purpose is a living thing – which is why an organization's life is derived from it. So, I suppose you could say, most organizations really need to get a life!

CHAPTER 7

Is Anybody Listening?

Yesterday, upon the stair,
I met a man who wasn't there
He wasn't there again today
I wish, I wish he'd go away...

— HUGH MEARNS, ANTAGONISH

Marketers, as a whole, tend to present content and channel as if they are enough, in and of themselves. Say the right thing, at the right time, with the right frequency on Facebook (or whatever the channel flavor of the week is,) and the customer will be beating down your door, *they* tell us. I propose "*they*" are wrong. *They* are missing the most crucial factor in this formula – and it is the factor that is giving marketing a bad name – the fact is that not every concept can capture the consumer's attention and interest, despite an alluring, well-timed, perfectly placed marketing communication. Lipstick, meet pig!

If you are not interested in pigs as a paramour, no amount of lipstick will make the pig appealing as a paramour. No

Facebook feed will turn your head. No "Friends of Pigs" group on LinkedIn, no "Lonely Pigs" billboard, or "Pigs Looking for Love" late night commercial will make you change your mind.

For a laughable moment, let's just suppose someone was foolish (and funded) enough to do this. It would become a joke. People would talk derisively about it, and tweet memes about it. There would be all manner of press about it. There would probably be a trial, covered on CNN, where the Pig Pimp is found guilty of animal abuse, in Pig Pimp vs. PETA. Still, only the profoundly weird would be interested in the actual "product", and they are not nearly a large enough market (we hope) to bail him/her out of this expensive campaign. Unfortunately for the pigs, and for our waistlines, most people are far more interested in killing and eating them, than loving them. This may change, but for now, that is the reality.

Now, if our friend, the Pig Pimp, were to shift slightly, and to present his pigs as pets, not paramours, and to showcase the animals' natural cognitive abilities which are demonstrably higher than a dog's or chimpanzee's (demonstrating its house-breakability, trainability, capacity to play video games, affectionate nature, compatibility with other animals and children – all of which are proven through numerous research studies – and throw in a dose of how   adopting these intelligent and affectionate animals as pets also saves our environment (factory farming is arguably the largest single contributor to our environmental issues worldwide – assuming you subscribe to the scientific studies that support climate change, of course) then what he has done is take the self-same product, and present it for an entirely different use – one whose time may just have arrived. This is, in fact, what organizations such as PETA and Mercy for Animals are doing today, and interestingly, the population claiming vegetarianism or veganism as their primary diet has doubled globally in the past decade. These organizations, while facing a great deal of derision both for their viewpoints and their tactics, have found a Purpose, stuck to it, and are seeing the results of their commitment.

What's extremely important to note in the case of PETA, Mercy for Animals, and the International Humane Society, is that they actually share a common Purpose. They each have a different approach, and they each serve a slightly different market, but their common Purpose is to elevate consciousness of the rampant abuse of animals worldwide, and shift society's behaviors and choices that have been made based on both very old, deep assumptions about animals along with fairly recent cultural excesses. What they are selling is individual funding to help raise additional awareness and help as many animals as possible escape (what they define to be) unusual and cruel conditions. Are they competing with each other? I don't think I am alone in my personal unwillingness, in the scenario of similar competing entities (take Salvation Army and Goodwill

Industries if you find animal welfare too controversial) to fund more than one that speaks to my heart. So, the competition for our hearts is intense in the non-profit sector, especially between those with shared, albeit real, Purpose.

So, now apply this scenario to a for-profit realm. I don't need more than one dry cleaner, primary care practitioner, cell service provider, nor do I need more than one electricity provider. I also don't actually need more than one grocery store, more than one church, more than one bank, and so on. Yet, like most everyone in the Western World, when it comes to certain things like groceries, I am willing to shop around for price and variety of offerings, as well as to have more than one provider in some specialized offerings.

Most heads of household regularly shop at two or three different groceries. They like the freshness of the produce at this store, the price of organic foods at the other, the variety of brands at another, and the proximity of yet another to their work. Not insignificantly, when they are short on time, they stop at the most convenient one, and settle for less than their preference in several areas. The same "grocery store" principle applies to the cell, bank and electricity providers, but the variation here is there is a greater built-in inertia with customer contracts and the lack of immediacy available for desired change without penalty. In these cases, the choice is made for a longer duration, and the discomfort and frustration must become higher to change – not because of the loyalty, but because of the difficulty.

With doctors, drycleaners, and other service providers (like landscapers, marketing agencies, hair stylists, etc.) there is also the issue of, "but they know me, and it will take a great deal of risk and potential effort on my part to teach a new provider my unique issues and preferences." Marketing in these situations is based on awareness (location, visibility, word of mouth referrals, and personal relationships.)

These practical, difficult-to-track choices are universal in the First World, where we have the greatest access to resources in recorded history, and the greatest perception of limitation on our own personal access to them – most especially our insatiable hunger for time and material goods which feel universally (and falsely) insufficient in these cultures. Marketing has created this mess, and in the process has made it extremely difficult for organizations of any size to market effectively and rise above the noise of same, same, same.

What's lost is true difference of Purpose. What is gained is an interesting phenomenon of creating false differentiation to manufacture need. The result is layers of confusion to both consumers and sellers alike of what is a true need and what is a manufactured need. It's no wonder that most sellers feel a certain level of fear about connecting with their target market effectively.

Here are a couple of manufactured needs that are so clever, most of us are not aware of them, or are only becoming aware of them. Ironically, they also no longer serve the entities that created them:

The first manufactured need is the differentiation between boys and girls baby clothes' colors. Originally clothing was neutral. Pastel colors became assigned as baby clothing colors in the mid-19th century – but not as gender identifiers.

In a June 1918 article from the trade publication *Earnshaw's Infants' Department* said, "The generally accepted rule is pink for the boys, and blue for the girls. The reason is that pink, being a more decided and stronger color, is more suitable for the boy, while blue, which is more delicate and dainty, is prettier for the girl." At that time, there were a number of differing opinions on the matter, ranging from sources which said blue was flattering for blonds, pink for brunettes; or blue was for blue-eyed babies, pink for brown-eyed babies.

In 1927, *Time Magazine* printed a chart showing sex-appropriate colors for girls and boys according to leading U.S. stores. In Boston, Filene's told parents to dress boys in pink. So did Best & Co. in New York City, Halle's in Cleveland and Marshall Field in Chicago. It wasn't until the 1940s that the current assignment of blue and pink settled in to a solid pattern, as decided by department stores, most of whom are no longer in business.

While the color of infant clothing is not the cause of confusion, it is indicative of the arbitrary nature of fashion today. The majority of the populace claims to loathe the mall phenomenon, but not enough to put a stop to the endless list of fashion retail chains that continues to grow and vie for a spot in the market, which is indicative of our cultural confusion. Each of these retailers struggles to differentiate in the realm of Purpose, competing instead for this market segment or that market segment like the sharks in a feeding frenzy. The stakes are high (revenue,) the competition is fierce, the stress is off the charts, and the idea of Purpose is lost. What has happened is the stores have created shorter "seasons" with smaller collections, and are vying to get to market faster than their competition. Thus, a fashion retailer races to keep ahead, when the average lifespan of one of these store concepts, if it is successful, is roughly 10 years on average.

The second, more widely known manufactured need, is the artificial combination of ingredients that is also highly addictive – sugar, fat and salt. This combination exists nowhere in nature, and that is, quite simply, because we do not need it. Just the opposite is true. We need to steer clear of it if we value our health. The initial hook was convenience – the convenience of prepared foods that fill the majority of shelves, even in purportedly "healthy" groceries, as well as convenience snacks, omnipresent fast food. The remaining hook is three-fold: these goods are prominent, lower cost, and addictive. The net damage in healthcare costs, medical debt and debilitating illnesses such as diabetes, clogged arteries, colitis, irritable bowel syndrome, and some believe, even cancer, are incalculable.

The initial push for these foods en masse occurred in the 50's, and it is only through consumer pressure and the rise of a new, Purpose-driven set of alternatives, that this manufactured need is being gradually shelved – if you will pardon the pun. Consumers like to congratulate themselves for their demand driving the rise of organics, natural foods, raw food, whole foods, and easy-to-prepare, natural meals. However, the availability and awareness of these offerings is what drove the demand, after 60 years – an entire generation – of the deadly trio of sugar/salt/fat being the predominantly most accessible option available.

Ironically, it is a fashion brand, Spanx, that has been the stand-out, Purpose-driven fashion brand, designed to address the need of camouflaging our perceived poor body shape, that has become this decade's Kleenex, or Coke. Also, *not* ironically, McDonald's is in a downward spiral, as a brand that has been the equivalent term for fast food for decades. It is unlikely that it will be able to shift this perception successfully, as culturally ingrained as it is -- especially now that it has upped the excess of the Big Mac with its Grand Mac. So far their advertising the health benefits of Egg McMuffins, or presenting fruit as sides, will shift this in consumers' minds at this point. The reason is simple – McDonald's has never had consumer health at the core of its Purpose. Its Purpose has been low-cost convenience. If McDonald's can take a long, searching look at its base assumptions, and turn convenience into real healthy alternatives that are also convenient, it *might* be the turn-around company of our lifetime. However, as long as the Big Mac, Quarter Pounder, sugary soft drinks, and "Super Size" menu remains, McDonald's days are numbered – as are most other fast food concepts that trade in the deadly three – salt, sugar and fat.

McDonald's has become the Pig Paramour. We just aren't interested. But what does interest consumers? That's the question all marketers want to know. Most marketers don't have the means for true market research studies, as mentioned earlier, but they cannot help but want access to the data the studies purport to provide.

Recently, however, some very high profile consumer research, in the form of electorate pre-election polling, proved wildly inaccurate, and a few decades ago so did the consumer studies around New Coke, another high profile missed mark. These were arguably statistically accurate populations that should, even with a variance, been on track. What went wrong? Consumers either misrepresented their preferences, or the surveys were poorly constructed. This author proposes that the electorate and New Coke research participants misrepresented themselves. As the old business saying goes, "Buyers are liars," and they lied.

The question about the reason for their lying could be the subject of an entire additional book. What is likely is that there were a number of reasons – the same reasons that people lie about anything:

1. They have some shame or uncertainty about their thoughts or actions.
2. They did think one way and then changed their minds.
3. They have intent to overpower, outwit, and even harm through subterfuge.
4. They do not want to experience consequences for their actions.
5. They hope to protect another from emotional or physical pain (altruism.)
6. They are sociopathic.

For both research polling instances cited above, it is likely that only #1 and #2 came into play, but that was all it took.

These are unusual cases, but they are significant in a number of ways – the most important of which is momentum. It is the power of the masses. Today it is easier than ever to build momentum through social media and it is easier than ever for it to dissipate exactly the way it came. All it takes is a small number of raving fans, as the book of the same name advocates, and the masses will follow. Equally, all it takes is a small number of angry detractors or thoroughly unenthusiastic non-advocates to eviscerate a brand.

The problem is getting that magical momentum going, and then maintaining it. The most successful momentum builders leverage the power of live experiences to keep it going. Energy in a group environment is one of the most powerful forces there is. It is also dangerous, and can be used for destructive purposes as easily as for constructive ones.

Many public, political and spiritual leaders have leveraged momentum successfully – from Martin Luther King to Adolf Hitler, and from Joel Olsteen to Kim Kardashian. Also, many brands have done it as well – brands like Google, Etsy, and Fitbit. Naturally, every brand wants that level of momentum and success, and they test the waters with customer surveys, assiduously studying the efforts of those companies and trying to emulate them. However, the new brand is not the older brand, and it needs to own its unique appeal. Generating awareness of a large target market, cultivating raving fans among early adopters in the target market, and the resulting momentum from brand interaction are the focus of marketing. However, the crucial components of timing, and fickle public opinion are wild cards that actually cannot be strategically managed. That is another controversial statement that many professional marketers are going to try to skewer me over. I challenge those marketers to carry the burden of proof that time and opinion can be managed with any predictable consistency. Instead those factors fall into that category of luck that most marketers would prefer business owners believe is a myth. Not every brand can nor will stand out at the level of the top 1% of visibility regardless of what they do, no matter how well they are funded, and how brilliant their offering.

If that depresses you, here's some good news: unwavering commitment to your brand *and its authentic Purpose* over a longer period of time (which varies wildly from 2-15 years, depending on the entity) with funding and a loyal initial client base, is almost guaranteed to generate the desired momentum tipping point. The key is that you look for a pattern of growth, not an overnight sensation. The result is some will vault into the 1%, while others will cruise in the top 10% or even top 20%. Ultimately, it isn't about the percentage you run with, it's whether you are running where your Purpose carries the most impact.

CHAPTER 8

Sharpening the Razor's Edge

"The sharp edge of a razor is difficult to pass over; thus the wise say the path to Salvation is hard."

— THE UPANISHAD

In the previous chapter we looked at how brand success is not entirely within an organization's control, and the crucial importance of staying true to your Purpose and commitment even though the process can, at times, be lengthy and arduous. We all would rather have the overnight success, and feel that somehow we have missed a crucial class in marketing somewhere when it doesn't happen immediately for us. We can be too quick to question our approach, our product, our research, and our branding. We have come to the razor's edge.

This anxiety leads to a desire to redirect our branding by questioning if it is really the right look and message for who we truly are. There is a common rule of thumb in marketing that a brand should undergo a "refresh" every two years. This continuous rebranding is one of the biggest scams in marketing today. The reasons for this vary from agency to agency, but most reasons fall into the following categories:

1. **Your brand looks old and outdated.**

   While it is possible that a company has not refreshed its logo and appearance in decades, and equally possible that its initial branding was already dated or off-message when it was launched, rebranding every two years to look absolutely current is the epitome of foolishness. If your brand is anachronistic, odds are you already know it, and you should absolutely do something about it, irrespective of years that have elapsed.

   On the other hand, rebranding like you were updating your wardrobe is not only an unnecessary expense; it is confusing to your customers. Customers want to be able to identify you easily, and a new look every two years is the antithesis of ease. Therefore, if you are being told to rebrand simply because time has elapsed and technology and consumers have changed *radically* over the past two years, get a second opinion.

2. **Your branding is inconsistent.**

   Inconsistent branding means an incoherent message to customers. Messaging and imagery together create an impression of strength, reliability, and Purpose regardless of whether you are a mom and pop drycleaner or the latest tech brand. However, this is still not necessarily a reason to do a complete rebrand when you may simply need to circle the wagons and clean up your communications. Don't throw the proverbial baby out with the bath water.

3. **You want to create "buzz" and get people talking about your brand (again.)**

This is the most ridiculous reason to rebrand I have heard, and I hear it over and over. Who "buzzes" about rebranding? Agencies, that's who! Unless you do something downright offensive, hilarious, risqué, or bizarre with your branding, the customers *are* likely to notice, but certainly not "buzz" about it. The intention in this line of reasoning is that customers get brand fatigue, and are on the lookout for things that are fresh and new. That does not require a rebrand, however. A new ad spot, or product line are not rebranding. Don't confuse the two. Customers, if they are loyal to your brand are far less concerned about your look than the interaction and benefit they have with your brand.

4. **The market has changed.**

Now, *this* could be a reason to rebrand. When your particular market and all that that entails (customer base, driving technologies and buying patterns) change, it is probably time to revamp your brand and your go-to-market strategy. What that means again, varies wildly and would be a book of its own. Some brands take market shifts and leverage themselves as a "so retro we're cool" brand, while others simply add an app and raise their visibility in other channels.

5. **Your offerings have changed.**

    Again, this is not necessarily a reason to rebrand. Hopefully, if you have added products you are checking them against your assumption audit and your Purpose as an organization. However, companies add new offerings every single day without the slightest impact to their overall branding. If the product affects the overall company target market and go-to-market strategy, then by all means, revamp the brand. If not, then stay the course, and for goodness sake, don't get distracted by pretty, shiny newness.

Rebranding is necessary if your branding is no longer an accurate reflection of your brand, or if you basically botched your branding initially. Numerous companies do actually have a botched brand, and only a handful are willing to acknowledge that their branding is a problem. One noteworthy example is an international technology company that spent, at a minimum, hundreds of thousands of dollars refreshing their brand. They did customer research, developed a new tagline, font family, color palette, and extensive image library. They developed videos, website updates, presentation templates, brochures, flyers, banners, intra-office refurnishing and graphics, and then went on a worldwide tour to all their offices to explain the new brand to all the employees, and generate buy-in. The new brand was months and months in the making, and to be fair, the rebranding work was coherent, consistent, intensely thought out and quite attractive.

I was fortunate enough to hear the customer research results. In it was an extremely thorough set of data filled with the feedback of those who knew the company best (customers) sharing their view of the company as stodgy, complex and frequently unreliable. Taking this input, and their intention to shift customer perception nearly 180 degrees, the company, and their agency, developed a very detailed rationale behind each of their branding changes. The final result was rainbows and bubbles.

Sit with that for a moment. If you were a customer, and you had real-time issues with a company that was, or wanted to be, providing your business-critical technology and they were living in the past, spending an inordinate amount of time dealing with errors, and their solution was a convoluted one at best; then the company shows up one day with rainbows and bubbles on all their materials – what would you think? That they had lost their fragile grip on reality? That they were spending their money in all the wrong places, perhaps? How about that you needed to find a different partner who dealt with their internal culture and processes, instead of creating an aspirational appearance that was dissonant with their approach!

The problem wasn't actually with their research. The survey results were an *excellent* reflection of reality, and told the company precisely what they needed to do with their brand – and they heard it and acknowledged the problem. Their reaction, however, was to precede any actual transformation with the appearance of one. This is the absolute *worst* approach to rebranding possible. If they had miraculously changed all their internal issues overnight so that the new branding was representative of true transformation within the organization, it could have been, arguably, a decent rebrand – if you embrace bubbles and rainbows, of course. The reality is, they didn't make that radical shift. They did, however keep their new brand, and perhaps, eight years later, their internal dynamics are catching up. Whether they are or not, backing into a cultural shift though a face-lift is not a terribly reliable way to raise market share, and it is never a reason to rebrand. It is worse, in fact, than the company that refuses to rebrand in spite of a need to.

So what happens when we come up to that razor's edge? What is the razor and what is the Salvation from a marketing perspective? I propose that the razor is an organization's Purpose, which we have already spent a good amount of time exploring. Salvation is seeing that Purpose fulfilled. That razor's edge is so inherently difficult to cross because an organization will inevitably struggle with constant internal and external forces that want to shape and alter the Purpose. Course corrections are always necessary, but now imagine trying to make them amid the speed and turbulence of a class five rapids. You really need to know what you are doing to not react rashly and flounder dangerously. A good guide who has done this before is a great asset, and allegedly, marketing can be precisely the guide to get us through the rapids.

A marketing "Sherpa" knows the pitfalls, how to avoid them, and where you need to go. Succinctly put – a marketing Sherpa knows *their* Purpose to help you achieve *yours*. Now here's where it gets interesting. There is almost no agreement among marketers about what their Purpose actually is. There are a lot of great Purposes for marketing which include:

- Attract attention and create interest.
- Drive traffic, leads, and sales (profits.)
- Identify the specific goals and needs of customers and to guide the creation of products or services to fulfill them.
- Find and keep customers.
- Lower the risk for the prospect to take the next step in the decision-making or buying process.
- Prove expertise.

Many are fond of quoting business writer and sage, Peter Drucker, with his famous (and somewhat obtuse) quote on the nature of marketing:

"Because the purpose of business is to create a customer, the business enterprise has two - and only two basic functions: marketing and innovation. Marketing and innovation produce results; all the rest are costs. Marketing is the distinguishing, unique function of the business."

But what does that *mean*?

It means marketing's purpose is, quite simply, to simultaneously reflect and embody the entity's Purpose. It matters not one, tiny bit whether the entity is an independent massage therapist or a Fortune 100 corporation. Each touch, communication, and interaction is either creating a brand in the customer's mind, or assimilating and adapting to the customer's reaction. This is a continuous feedback loop that is never-ending, until and unless the entity ceases to exist by virtue of its failure to fulfill either its own Purpose or the needs of its customers.

So, yet again, we come face to face with the truth we often prefer to resist and deny: we must be our own Sherpa. Sure, we can have those who expand our reach and accelerate our ability to act through sheer numbers, and perhaps specific expertise in how to apply certain media, channels or content. Ultimately, a great marketer knows their Purpose better than anyone, and all those helpers are only helping so long as they fully understand that Purpose as well.

That list of very specific purposes for marketing – from awareness to driving profits – really are all equally valid, depending on circumstances. Yet they are also equally meaningless if the organization is without a macro-Purpose behind it all.

CHAPTER 9

This is Personal

"Example is not the main thing influencing others. It is the only thing."

— ALBERT SCHWEITZER

It doesn't matter how hard you try to be objective, your marketing will reflect your personal bias and preferences. Essentially, you will eventually be authentic, whether you like it or not. It might be trendy or traditional, social or print, but your marketing will have your DNA all over it. The reason this is so important to understand is that when we try to deny it, we sabotage the crucial messages we need to deliver.

Brand personality is defined as the way a brand speaks and behaves. In other words, we assign human personality characteristics to a brand. Most marketers exploring a brand's personality will ask you to think about how your brand ought to be perceived by your target audience and how it ought to make them feel. This is correct, procedurally, but interestingly, it is often approached backwards.

The most common way we undercut our brand personality through our marketing is by trying to reflect our customers' personalities back to them in an effort to be an empathetic brand, before we have clarified what *our* personality is. While that is an understandable approach, which many people use on a one-on-one personal level, in order to create instant synergy, it is not sustainable the deeper the relationship becomes. It is, ultimately false. When a customer catches on to the dissonance between your inauthentic message and the true personality (yours) behind your brand, and feels the dissonance is too great, the relationship will soon be over, try though you might to change to please them, much like a bad marriage.

A far more sustainable version of this is to invert it. Be proud of your brand's personality. Put it out there for all to see in its unadulterated glory. Then trust that the customers who identify with you will embrace it fully. In other words, treat your brand with the same regard and sense of value as you (hopefully) would yourself, trusting that those who truly appreciate you for your unique style exist in abundance, because if they don't, you are in for an uphill climb regardless.

So what happens when you attract the customers that aren't in alignment with your brand personality? Hopefully you do two things immediately:

1. Recognize you are not a fit, and if you are in a position to do so, redirect them to another offering that is.
2. Ask them specifically why they chose you (a cross-check on your messaging and channels) and then address anywhere the disconnect might have originated at your end.

Instead, countless companies do two very different things:

1. Explain to the customer that they really *must* want what the organization is providing.
2. Try to be what the customer is seeking, regardless of alignment with the actual brand Purpose.

The reason companies are so afraid to send a bad fit packing (lovingly, of course) is the belief that their brand is lacking in some way – most especially in an abundance of customers that are actually a good fit. These organizations actually have low self-esteem, if you can believe it. They might even look strong and secure on the surface, but underneath they are frightened and needy, and unable to tolerate rejection.

It seems so unnecessary to tell an organization to believe in itself, but all you have to do is look at the bad reputation salespeople have gotten, and you can't help but know it is because so many of them are out there selling to anyone they think might buy, regardless of any alignment with the organization. The resulting conflict, where the sales person pursues and the prospect deflects is exhausting to everyone involved, and has a depressing affect on the entire organization.

It is because this very scenario still plays out over and over, that I am giving high marks to the Sandler Method of sales, where the objective is to get to a "no," instead of "yes," thus identifying that there is not a synergistic need, and saving everyone a tremendous amount of time and heartache.

The Blame Game

Successful brands start and end with the brand. It is true that a Purpose-driven brand must have a target customer who needs it, but if it doesn't, then something is askew with its Purpose. It is just a brand contemplating its navel.

The willingness to look inward for what is right and wrong, and adjust as an organization grows, is a universal indicator of longevity and brand strength. It isn't the market. It isn't customers. It isn't the absence of the latest innovation from its competitor. It is a brand that has a Purpose to fulfill, and by goodness, it is going to do just that.

Struggling organizations that point the finger at consumer spending, the cost of employee wages and healthcare, the cost of goods and manufacturing, the underhanded dealings of their competitors, the unethical practices of their customers (seriously, get a new customer!) the pressures of the market, the poor decisions by previous management, the fickle nature of customers, and an endless list of other pressures, are headed for disaster. They are attempting to side-step personal responsibility for their own success (or failure.) It is that simple. Any organization that assumed that ideal conditions were critical to their success has a feeble Purpose at best.

Conditions can be excruciatingly challenging in business and life, and we are not ever going to be able to failsafe our approach – with one exception – the use of our innate ability to adapt. Companies that hold to their Purpose and innovate in response to conditions instead of wringing their hands and railing against reality at least are on their way to regaining their traction. That's not to say that advocating for better conditions is not a valid tool in one's arsenal, but to play the victim is organizational suicide.

As Ayn Rand's says, "The question isn't who's going to let me; it's who's going to stop me." Thus, companies that are awake and aware of the challenges they face, and adapt to them boldly with creativity and strength, are the ones that provide inspiration to their employees, their customers, and anyone who is watching. They also have a remarkably attractive marketing story to tell, and should do so at every opportunity. However, in this pressurized scenario, marketing can only follow the lead of the organization and reflect it and project it. Marketing can't create the solution to the problem that it didn't create. Therefore, no organization can realistically market its way out of a challenging situation, although many have tried.

There is also a darker and pervasive saboteur of brand success that falls squarely on the shoulders of the organization – and that is its internal ethical standards. So many companies today have a list of core values, but few of them make it a point to instill them and use them as guideposts for the work they do. Therefore, they are meaningless and trite.

Whether it is a result of these meaningless values, or the cause of their lack of meaning, an unfortunate number of business people today have become grossly cynical, stating, "The end justifies the means." That little statement originates with Niccolò Machiavelli in his seminal work, *The Prince,* which is a blueprint for how to attain and retain power – at all costs. As a quick primer (if you have forgotten your 10th grade studies) the ethics our "Prince" would need to apply would be the following:

- It is better to be stingy than generous.
- It is better to be cruel than merciful.
- It is better to break promises if keeping them would be against one's interests.
- Princes must avoid making themselves hated and despised; the goodwill of the people is a better defense than any fortress.
- Princes should undertake great projects to enhance their reputation.
- Princes should choose wise advisors and avoid flatterers.

This Prince values one, and only one, thing: power. How positively *medieval*! Yet I have watched numerous executives do many or most of these things without batting an eye, even though, post-Enlightenment, we would prefer to flatter ourselves that we value many things, such as collaboration, communication, commitment, trust, integrity, honesty, love, justice, compassion, abundance, happiness, freedom, health, innovation, and, depending on the person or organization, hundreds more.

Research tells another story. Out of 120 million people in the workplace in the United States alone, at least half of us have been shocked to witness unexpected and unethical behaviors, from illicit affairs, to drugs and alcohol, theft, misuse of company privilege or authority, lying, insider trading, under the table dealings, and outright unlawful activities. Some studies say 60 million of us have personally witnessed such actions in our own workplace. With those sort of numbers, we are not so very far removed from our Prince's activities at all, and the results are frustrating at best, and frightening at worst.

I propose that Niccoló was actually very close to right, but still, very, very, very wrong, nonetheless. The end does not *justify* the means – the end *reflects* the means. One word changes everything. What we say, and how we act (the means) leaves an indelible impression on the result. Ill-gotten results do not hold up well to the test of time, and create a ripple effect that generates even greater conflict and discord, which is written large across our headlines, as well as in the rise and fall of major organizations every day.

If we are to claim to value things such as integrity, trust and collaboration – as most organizations today do claim in their "core values", we must embody those, not only personally, but professionally as well. The reason, psychologists agree, is that we, as humans, do register and recognize the dissonance between words and actions at a subconscious level, even if we don't on a conscious one. The result is a mistrust, and ultimately, a rejection of the individual or organization that is presenting the dissonance. This affects corporate culture as well as the relationship with customers. Get out of alignment with your employees and your customers and watch your market share shrink.

I actually had a business partner once who proudly affirmed his disdain for integrity in business. Needless to say, we are no longer business partners. When someone is willing to be unethical "just this once," or only in a certain aspect of their life, then two things happen: the first is their own boundaries begin to erode around what is personally (or organizationally) acceptable, and the second is that anyone who is aware of their lack of ethics in one area will presume they are at least capable of unethical behavior in other areas. The result is that the unethical person/organization loses credibility both with themselves and others. Any leverage or gratification they hoped to achieve in the process is always and forevermore at risk then, which is why we are so afraid to "get caught." Additionally, many recipients of unethical behavior will retaliate. This creates discord and distraction from any growth until the conflict is resolved. In short, unethical behavior sets up a lose-lose scenario that can be extremely difficult to end.

There's that saying, "If you can spot it, you got it." Anyone who witnesses unethical behavior is affected by it, even if, as many do, they turn a blind eye to it. We cannot un-see or un-know what we know. If we do not stand up and demand to be treated ethically, and that our coworkers and customers are also treated ethically, then we are just as unethical as the actual perpetrator in our complicity.

Of course, few, if any, of us are 100% in alignment with our personal ethics all the time, but if we value a relationship, we clean up our behavior right away, and don't repeat it. Companies can, and do, take this amending action as well when they slip. We make a correction because we realize that the prime reason for ethics, and societal rules of behavior, are to operate harmoniously for the benefit of the majority of parties involved, and this requires trust of intention of two very basic things: that we mean each other no harm, and that we are vested in the best interests of the other person.

Companies that do not understand the crucial importance of ethics to their success will find themselves continuously embattled and besieged. I will not claim that they will fall like the Walls of Jericho, because they don't always. Just looking at those earlier research numbers tells us Enron, Worldcom, Tyco along with JP Morgan Chase and Goldman Sachs can only be the tip of the iceberg. Still, they tend to overshadow companies that are being lauded as some of the most ethical companies today, such as Aflac, Fluor Corporation, GE, Milliken & Company, Starbucks and UPS.

Harvard Business School professor, and author of *High Commitment, High Performance*, Michael Beer makes a case for building companies that can perform at high levels for extended periods – and he directly ties this longevity to corporate ethics, citing a lack of higher purpose, clear strategy, and risk management as the main causes of Wall Street's abysmal failure in 2008.

Ethical companies do exist. They do flourish. They do have a stellar reputation, and that equates to a priceless marketing message: you can trust us. This means that they are not only *as likely* to flourish as a Machiavellian counterpart – they are potentially *more likely* to flourish.

CHAPTER 10

The Echo Chamber Is
A Pool Of Possibility

Life is an echo. What you send out comes back. What you sow, you reap. What you give, you get. What you see in others, exists in you.

— ZIG ZIGLAR

I was with a group of franchise CEOs not too long ago, and one of them was trying to determine how to create a social media meme to promote her brand. She had seen others generate big awareness and big brand loyalty through the use of memes, but she was mystified about how they started one. Just to be clear – memes are ideas spread "virally" from one person to another. Most include images or videos file, and, of course, social media is the perfect conduit for memes spreading like wildfire in just hours in some cases, and reaching exponentially more people. You can't buy that kind of marketing. It's priceless.

Most companies still struggle to get out of their outward-facing, company-centric message platform long enough to connect their offering with a societal pain (or laugh) point.

One that did, hit a good meme stride is Denny's, actually, with its spoof of gold iPhone 5's - sharing a picture of pancakes with the text "Pancakes" stylized like the iPhone advertisement, with smaller text reading, "Always available in golden." LOL.

But more often than not, meme marketing is still accidentally successful, rather than intentional. Who hasn't seen Euro RSCG Worldwide advertising campaign for Dos Equis? The ads featured actor Jonathan Goldsmith as "the most interesting man in the world." And now thousands and thousands of memers have hijacked the image, to the brand's enormous benefit, for the laughter generated by the familiar phrase, "I don't always…but when I do, it's…"

Despite what social media mavens tell us, the laws behind social media are still murky as…well…traditional media. Certainly there are best practices, and horrifically bad practices, but most brands will tell you they are in social media as a "price of poker" and not because they are reaping volumes of business from it. It is always touted as the low cost marketing alternative, and also the big time-suck as well.

That is not to say that marketers should stay away from social media. In fact, they would be well served to study it as they have never considered studying a channel before. The waves and swirls of public opinion they will find within this untamed wilderness are as unpredictable as the weather, but just as powerful. Social media has the power to reveal a culture's Purpose and its deepest dysfunctions, and thus a discerning brand can identify a jumping in point that makes enduring impact, if it knows its own authentic voice. But marketers have to be willing to stop observing from a distance, and instead immerse themselves in the madness of what it is to be social.

Many are beginning to refer to social media as an echo chamber, asserting that participants are not willing to interact with others of an opposing viewpoint, but instead just share and re-share the same old thoughts back and forth, over and over. My experience indicates that that is not entirely true. I believe social media is more of a ripple chamber. Someone with an agenda throws an idea out into the social sphere, and if it resonates with enough people (and their circle of influence is great enough) it has a strong share rate, which then goes out another circle and another and another, but gradually the ripple dies out – especially if it intersects with a strong, competing idea. As with life, the social sphere is wildly responsive to the following things:

1. Humor
2. Inspiration
3. Fear
4. Self-identification
5. Comfort
6. Awe
7. Domination/Righteousness

Sometimes the response is utter rejection, but the group is larger than the whole, and tends to move in mass, until someone pitches in an original idea that strikes a new nerve, and sending the wave of conversation swirling elsewhere. Every person present in the social sphere is a marketer of something – even if it is only the delightful nature of their children, which is what professional marketers must understand they are competing with. In the social world, marketing is literally a sidebar to the conversation that is also a type of marketing, the feed. Marketers want to be de-marginalized (taken off the sidebar) and introduced into the conversation in the feed. Very few ever are unless they pay top dollar or something goes awry (Starbucks red holiday cup in 2014, as referenced earlier, for instance) or the brand is being sold by Facebook users like LulaRoe, dōTERRA, or Rodan+Fields. Brand marketing is by its nature removed from the personal conversation, and unless you stumble onto a magical meme, there's no altering that fact.

All this is to say, don't steer clear of social media. Far from steering clear, be engaged with your customers everywhere and in every way possible. It's important. It matters that you are where they are. That's just part of being a good brand for your customers – that is, if you are listening as much as you are talking. Customers want to feel that as a brand, you hear them and identify with them. The only way to do that is to engage them where they, their friends and their families live. Short of moving into their homes, social media is the next best thing.

Now here is the trick, which it appears very few on social media – either users or brands – have caught onto: Stop listening *only* to self-identifiers. If we are only willing to hear what we already think we know, no growth is possible. No personal growth is possible, and no brand growth is possible. Many, many brands survey their customers at various touch points in the customer experience, and determine where the process is working or in need of improvement. On the other hand, it would be unrealistic in most cases for brands to attempt to gather any sort of information from non-customers in any sort of meaningful way, since there is no motivation to collaborate outside of the relationship with the brand.

This is where social media comes in. Beneath the time investment of just the daily postings and ad spots, there is a deeper time commitment – get to know the customers who like you. Then determine not just who they are, but also who they are not. What do they self-identify with, and what do they reject as unlike themselves? When you do this, you are holding up a mirror to your brand that shows you whether you have appealed to all or only some of who you think you are. Are you demonstrating your Purpose clearly? Are you even reaching your intended customer?

Social media is good for a great number of things – not only pushing out messages, but also actively listening to everything swirling around you in its messy, noisy, vibrant, ever-changing landscape. This is a place where, once we are present, it is very, very hard to hide. Use that to your best advantage by entering into the fray actively, with a bilateral approach, since many times the best marketers, like the best leaders, listen more than they speak.

While many individuals are feeling overwhelmed and anxious recently as a result of social media, there is a fascinating phenomenon I believe more and more are catching onto – and it is to understand that the echo chamber is more than that. It is a dynamic system where anyone can tap into the mass psyche with a well-timed and sympathetic idea, which will become the new echo. I experienced this recently in the swirl of post-election angst. I certainly had my opinions, as did everyone. Some were silent, some abandoned the social media ship, but others, like myself, began reframing the conversation in an affirmative way, rather than defining what we were against. We spoke in terms of what we stood for and refused to argue, but we did not refuse to listen to those who disagreed with our views – instead we asked questions like, "Tell me more about that." What happened next, in my little experiment, was nothing less than incredible. My posts were picked up by friends and reposted, then their friends reposted, and outward ripples went on beyond my ability to measure. I had people Instant Messaging me, and others were personally pulling me aside to thank me – on both sides of the debate. There were even people I didn't know trying to friend me specifically for that reason. It altered my view of social media forever.

My little social experiment let me see these media in an entirely new light – the light that shines for every brand all the time – the light that illuminates a real need in the sphere in which it operates. The brand that intends to grow must be listening, not to the echo chamber of its own feedback loop, but to the vibrations of change that are always happening around it. No brand can create a solely self-serving meme, push it out, and expect it to resonate. Yet, if a brand is attending very carefully, it can hear the yearning of its audience for something new – something that helps, comforts or heals. Brands that do address this are transformed forever.

CHAPTER 11

The Marathon Brand

I wish to do something Great and Wonderful, but I must start by doing the little things like they were Great and Wonderful.

— ALBERT EINSTEIN

One thing none of us are able to manage with any consistency is timing. We certainly can affect it, but control it reliably? Never. However we certainly do try, to our endless frustration and ultimate exhaustion. An exhausted brand team is not going to be a very successful brand team but I watch them every day in company after company racing against the powerful and invisible deadline. Brand success is still measured by RevPAR and speed far more often than on longevity and endurance. After all, who wants to wait for what they want in any area? Why should business be different? We could discuss why this is the case all day long, but ultimately, it all comes down to the belief we all culturally seem unwilling to surrender, that speed and volume create a momentum that ends in endurance, while reality has not born this belief out in the slightest.

Our business culture lauds the "fast-growth" companies, and attempts divine their secrets and to emulate them, while most of them actually do not endure for very long. A 2015 joint study between The Kauffman Foundation and *Inc. Magazine* looked at the fastest growing companies, and discovered that about two-thirds of the companies that made the list had shrunk in size, gone out of business, or been disadvantageously sold. The research analysis determined that the failing two-thirds fell prey to the belief that financial viability was the end goal, and in a number of ways they abandoned the mature business process of ensuring constant innovation and change. In short, they were victims of their own definition of success, which lacked the essential quality of a defining Purpose.

In its report, inflammatorily entitled "Grow Fast or Die Slow," McKinsey & Company asserted that, in fact, roughly 85 percent of what they called "super growers" were unable to maintain their growth rates. In the same article, they proposed there was a proven recipe for sustainable fast growth, which involved the "right" market, monetization model, rapid adoption, stealth, and incentives (although they do not explain how each of those play a part nor the correct manner in which to implement them.) They then added a very important caveat: "Pitfalls include transitioning at the wrong time and selecting the wrong strategy…" In other words, the recipe is not so proven if we can dismiss those who disprove the principle by simply asserting their timing and strategy were off.

Interestingly, McKinsey & Company did not explore the "Die Slow" part of their title. The reason is because that is not necessarily the alternative to rapid growth. An endless array of articles stream forth every year from *Forbes, Inc.* and other business observers beating the drum of slow and steady growth. *Inc. Magazine* spells it out as plainly as one can imagine in "Sustained Growth Predicts Business Success," by Executive Editor, Scott Lieb, saying, quite simply, "The only statistically significant predictor of a company's future success is steady growth; short- and even long-term bursts mean almost nothing." He goes on to add, "Studying company performance over a 20-year span, we also found that the faster a company grew in one period, the less likely it was to grow again in the future (and the more likely it was to fail.)"

Even as the failed business body pile mounts daily, the myth of fast-growth being equivalent to success persists. Pressure from investors and shareholders looking for a fast return, as well as the attraction of top new talent hires, and of course, the delightful ego boost each are all very tempting incentives to grow, and grow fast. Even data like California State University finance professor Cyrus Ramezani's analysis of the relationship between growth and shareholder value, which concluded that the companies with the fastest revenue growth (average annual sales growth of 167% over a 10-year period) returned the worst share price performance during that same time period than slower growing firms (average growth of 26%) still doesn't dissuade the entrepreneurs from trying. Most companies want to be the exception, and believe that they can.

I am a fan of being an exception that disproves the rule myself. However, we don't do that by trying the same old things and expecting different results. Obviously, those attempting fast-growth are floundering on the endurance test. Like Icarus, they are flying too close to the sun with wings of wax. So, once again, we find ourselves facing a crossroads where something is amiss in the assumptions. A company can be all about the financial boon for them and their stakeholders, but not at the exception of the rest of the equation. Again, money solely for money's sake is a fool's errand, and will end with same emptiness as motivated it.

The companies that are in this for the long-haul are also overwhelmingly in it for the benefit of the multitude. They understand that "they" are a part of the "we" collective. As a result, they are consciously taking measures (which might slow them down in some cases) to protect their product's integrity, continue their focus on innovation, and safeguard their company culture, which once damaged, can rapidly undermine the entire organization. In fact, even those rare, fast-growth companies that managed to last over time, attribute their success to those same ideals: quality, innovation and culture. What's more, culture ranked highest of all. It is the keystone of every organization – and it, as we come full circle, is the essential ingredient in every piece of marketing.

Like Virgin CEO, Richard Branson, who I mentioned earlier, known for his employee-first management style, Warren Buffet is known for his stance regarding the unimpeachable impact of culture, 'Focus on your customers and lead your people as though their lives depended on your success." They are both wildly successful business men by any measure imaginable, and they are both right. Still there is another crucial component they have implied, but not directly addressed: happy employees are not happy for long without meaning and direction. It is in our nature.

It is also in our nature to desire immediate results, even to our own detriment, if we are afraid and/or uncomfortable, and one of our greatest points of discomfort is in the category of having enough – enough money, enough time, enough love, enough beauty, enough youth, enough health, enough stability, and on and on. This sense of scarcity even exists among the wealthiest of us, and it drives us to do hurtful things to ourselves, our relationships, our environment, our communities, and even our children's futures. The immediate fear feels much more real than the possible (likely) distant outcome. Take the epidemic of sleep deprivation our entire world is suffering under. Most of it is focused around the disproportionate demands of our work lives, from both self-imposed expectations, as well as corporate dictates. In her bestselling book, *The Sleep*

Revolution, Arianna Huffington does a remarkable job of making a case, in frightening detail, for not only the immediately devastating effects on our health from sleep deprivation, but also the damage done to creativity, innovation, endurance, impulse management, rational thought, decision making and every human function that is behind successful business endeavors. So, in our desire to do more as rapidly as possible, we actually are undoing ourselves irreparably.

What individuals experience in the microcosm, organizations are experiencing in the macrocosm. The demand for immediate and incredible results corrodes the organization from the inside out – or perhaps it manifests more like a comet that burns itself up in the atmosphere. Either way, the unnatural speed disallows natural resource replenishment that is required for sustainability. There are those that grow faster than others, but like Olympic athletes, they did not step onto the field untested, and they had already demonstrated an innate talent in that arena. Therefore, gazing at the accomplishments and speed of others is really a terrible measure of the natural speed and growth of your own organization.

Once again, it is important to recognize and embrace the inherent nature of who your organization is and it wants to become. If you cannot invest in your business for as long as is needed because you are underfunded, over-extended with investors, too caught up in tactics and not enough on

Purpose and vision, unwilling to be self-examining as well as listening to your customers, and flexible enough to adjust and adapt as your reality emerges, then perhaps you are not ready to really be what you claim you want to be. There is no shame in that. It is just an issue of timing and readiness. Instead of making your marketing a scapegoat, just close up shop, regroup, and try again when you *are* able and willing to do all those things.

But if you are ready to do this for as long as it takes – if you are committed to the process as much as the outcome – to your people, your product, and yes, your Purpose that you believe in, then walk confidently in the direction you have set. Trust your instincts, but get sound advice. Be confident enough to risk, and humble enough to admit when you made a mistake. Good marketing will reflect this mindset, but truly great marketing will help you create it.

ABOUT THE AUTHOR

Stacey Ruth is a highly acclaimed entrepreneur and marketer. Over the past 25 years she has accumulated numerous awards and certifications, including Certified ROI Professional, Top 50 Entrepreneurs by *Catalyst Magazine*, Top 100 Event Agencies by *Event Marketer Magazine*, Top Meeting Planners to Watch in *Convention South Magazine*. She has been a founding partner of two multi-million dollar agencies: The WOW Factory, and most recently, Actio Marketing. Through her experience with Fortune 1000 companies as well as start-ups, she has seen over and over again the common challenges every marketer faces, regardless of their level of expertise. She shares with organizations and individuals how skill can be meaningless when a sense of Purpose is lacking or discordant. Her unique technique of unearthing key assumptions that undermine success is truly remarkable, and she shares it through her books, her blog, Insight Out, her writing, her presentations and seminars, as well as one-on-one coaching.

www.ingramcontent.com/pod-product-compliance
Lightning Source LLC
Chambersburg PA
CBHW070934210326
41520CB00021B/6943